Books by Drew Kizer

Dangerous Playground

Christian Hope

The Cast of the Cross

From Conquerors to Kings

From Captives to Christ

Wisdom's Call

Make Your Stand

Christian Faith
Focusing on the One Who Makes All Things Possible

Drew Kizer

CHRISTIAN FAITH

Copyright © 2018 by Drew Kizer
6909 Timber Trail Road
Leeds, AL 35094

Published by Riddle Creek Publishing
320 Spring Cove Rd.
Florence, AL 35634
www.riddlecreekpublishing.com

Cover design by Patrick Burch

Unless otherwise indicated, all Scripture quotations are from The Holy Bible, English Standard Version, copyright © 2001 by Crossway Bibles, a division of Good News Publishers. Used by permission. All rights reserved.

ISBN: 9781718069671

CHRISTIAN FAITH

TABLE OF CONTENTS

Preface	1

THE MEANING OF FAITH
1. The Focus of Faith	5
2. Faith without God	17
3. Faith without Knowledge	31
4. Faith without Works	43

THE FIRST SOURCE OF FAITH: MIRACLES
5. The Reason for Miracles	57
6. A Believer's Unbelief	71
7. Long Distance Healing	81
8. Walking Trees	91
9. The Man Who Had Died	99

THE SECOND SOURCE OF FAITH: THE BIBLE
10. The Inspiration of the Bible	109
11. How to Study the Bible	121
12. Obedience through Suffering	131
13. Planting Faith	143

APPENDIX
14. The Holy Spirit	157
Endnotes	167

Faith is
not knowing what God will do,
but knowing He can do
anything.

PREFACE

> Now when Elisha had fallen sick with the illness of which he was to die, Joash king of Israel went down to him and wept before him, crying, "My father, my father! The chariots of Israel and its horsemen!" And Elisha said to him, "Take a bow and arrows." So he took a bow and arrows. Then he said to the king of Israel, "Draw the bow," and he drew it. And Elisha laid his hands on the king's hands. And he said, "Open the window eastward," and he opened it. Then Elisha said, "Shoot," and he shot. And he said, "The Lord's arrow of victory, the arrow of victory over Syria! For you shall fight the Syrians in Aphek until you have made an end of them." And he said, "Take the arrows," and he took them. And he said to the king of Israel, "Strike the ground with them." And he struck three times and stopped. Then the man of God was angry with him and said, "You should have struck five or six times; then you would have struck down Syria until you had made an end of it, but now you will strike down Syria only three times." (2 Kings 13:14-19)

Perhaps there is no better illustration of faith than this odd chapter in the life of Elisha. Everything you need to know about faith is packed into this perplexing tale.

Joash, king of Israel, visits an ailing Elisha. He is worried about Syria. We can assume he visited Elisha for guidance, but the prophet mystifies him by ordering the king to get a bow and arrows, draw the bow, and shoot eastward out the open window. As the stupefied king obeys,

Elisha makes him even more uncomfortable by laying his hands upon the king's. Joash came for advice, but he finds himself practicing archery instead.

Elisha then issues another order: "Take the arrows, and strike the ground with them." The king hesitantly drives three into the ground and returns Elisha's gaze while holding the remaining arrows in his hand. This drove Elisha to the edge. "You should have struck five or six times; then you would have struck down Syria until you had made an end of it, but now you will strike down Syria only three times!"

If we were not reading the Bible, we might think the author was trying too hard to be original. But the Holy Spirit has a reason for including this awkward scene between prophet and king.

Joash's faith was being tested. God did not come to him in an epiphany of angels singing "peace on earth" but through the words of a prophet. Also, the instructions Joash received were so counterintuitive, only someone who completely trusted God would comply with them. When the king halfheartedly shot a few arrows instead of eagerly emptying his quiver, it was clear that he was not on board. He was okay with God as long as He made sense. But what was this business of shooting perfectly good arrows into the ground? Joash was being tested, and he failed.

Abraham's sacrifice or Peter's call to come to Christ on the water might be more familiar, but Joash's test of faith seems to me to be closer to our experience. Unlike Abraham and Peter's tests, Joash risked nothing physically. At most, he would have wasted a few arrows. But spiritually, everything was at stake. Isn't this like God's beckoning us to baptism, a quiet dip into a pool of water with spiritual implications that extend into heaven itself? (Romans 6:3-4).

Or consider the Christian's responsibility to the poor. From an earthly vantage point, ignoring a need makes no difference to a person in a position to help, but from heaven's perspective, this kind of negligence condemns on Judgment Day (Matthew 25:31-46).

Joash did not understand why Elisha put his hands over his own when he drew back the bow, nor did he see the significance in throwing away his arrows. His job as king of Israel was not to understand these things, but to obey the Word of the Lord that had come through His prophet. Faith is not always understanding what God is up to. Faith is trusting Him enough to obey His Word no matter what He asks. Therefore, faith depends on a steadfast love for God. No one in his right mind would obey orders from a person he did not trust, especially when they made no sense. But if someone he loved said, "You know me. You love me. Do this. Trust me," he would act, even if he was bewildered. That's faith, the basis of the Christian experience.

ONE

THE FOCUS OF FAITH

One language held his heart and lip,
Straight onward to his goal he trod,
And proved the highest statesmanship
Obedience to the voice of God.

-John Greenleaf Whittier

Now more than ever, it is hard to stay focused on what is important. Brand strategist Cheryl Swanson says we are processing information at 400 times the rate of our Renaissance ancestors.[1] Another estimate has it that the world produced five exabytes of information in 2002. That is the same amount of information produced from the beginning of time through the year 2000.[2] With the proliferation of information increasing at this alarming rate, how are we to excise the nonessential, meaningless distractions away from our lives to get to what really matters?

A friend of mine shared an experience he had in a presentation that illustrates the way individuals and organizations lose focus. A senior executive presented a slide with writing on two sides of the screen. The left side of the screen read, "Brand (What We Stand For)." The right side of the screen read, "Reputation (What We Are Known For)." The executive asked, "What is the goal of our company?" She then advanced the slide so that an equal sign appeared between the two sides. "Our goal at a basic level," she said, "is for our reputation to be the same as our brand, for what we are known for to equal what we stand for."

Is that true in your life? Does your brand equal your reputation? When people think about you, does their idea of who you are match what you really stand for? Elders, what about your church? If your church is like mine, you have a purpose statement or some kind of biblical goal that has been set for your congregation. But does your reputation show that you have been able to focus on that goal? What does the community think about your congregation? Is its conception anywhere close to your ambition? Parents, what about your families? How close is your reputation to your ideals?

The distance between your brand and your reputation reveals the level of your focus. If we are being honest, some of us don't even have a brand; we don't have any idea what we stand for. The rest of us see some distance between what we stand for and what we are known for. The longer the distance, the less focused we are.

The church in Ephesus had lost its focus due to some influential teachers who were "swerving" and had "wandered away into vain discussion" (1 Timothy 1:6). They had veered so far off course that they had "made shipwreck of their faith" (v. 19). Their lack of focus had caused them to drift into two distractions Paul desperately wanted the church to avoid. The apostle writes to Timothy, saying,

> As I urged you when I was going to Macedonia, remain at Ephesus so that you may charge certain persons not to teach any different doctrine, nor to devote themselves to myths and endless genealogies, which promote speculations rather than the

stewardship from God that is by faith. (1 Timothy 1:3-4)

Paul calls the first of these distractions "any different doctrine." By now the apostles' teaching had developed by inspiration into a standard to be followed by the church as a whole. Since this teaching originated with God, it was to be taken seriously. No deviation was tolerated. In another place, Paul says,

> I am astonished that you are so quickly deserting him who called you in the grace of Christ and are turning to a different gospel.... [E]ven if we or an angel from heaven should preach to you a gospel contrary to the one we preached to you, let him be accursed. (Galatians 1:6, 8)

The second of these distractions is more difficult to define. Paul speaks of "myths and endless genealogies," which some scholars link to Gnostic heresies that may have already been incubating in the church at that time. But more likely, Paul refers to Jewish preoccupations that clouded the teaching of the church. In his letter to Titus, Paul urges Titus to rebuke elders who devote themselves to "Jewish myths" (Titus 1:14). The "endless genealogies" could refer to the way that some teachers would use the Old Testament genealogies for allegorical and legendary interpretations of the Scriptures.[3]

There are, indeed, plenty of Jewish fantasies that attempted to fill in the gaps left by divine revelation. The *Book of Jubilees* is an extensive retelling of Genesis and Exodus found among the Dead Sea Scrolls. The book claims that God revealed more to Moses on Mount Sinai than what is recorded in the Bible. It is exciting reading. An account of the angels' creation is given, along with four classifications: angels of the presence, angels of sanctification, guardian angels, and angels over nature. A group of fallen angels married female humans and brought forth a race of giants known as the Nephilim. If you have been wondering about Cain's wife, her name was Awan, and, yes, she was his sister. Events in the book follow a solar calendar, and dates and numbers are emphatic. The entire history of creation and Israel is given in divisions of forty-nine years each, or "jubilees." The elapsed time from the Creation to Mount Sinai is calculated as fifty jubilees, hence the name of the book.

A more familiar myth is *Additions to Esther*, contained in the Apocrypha. Have you ever wondered what happened when Esther came to see Ahasuerus without being called? The Bible says that Esther's visit to the king was risky, and if Ahasuerus had not extended his golden scepter to her she would have been put to death. Esther 5 tells us that when the king saw Queen Esther standing in the court, "she won favor in his sight, and he held out to Esther the golden scepter that was in his hand." Then Esther approached, touched the scepter, and made her request (Esther 5:1-3). Evidently, that was not enough detail for some of the Jews. In *Additions to Esther*, the Queen says, "I saw you, my Lord, like an angel of God, and my heart was shaking with fear at your glory. For you are wonderful, my Lord, and your countenance is full of grace." She then faints, and the king, agitated, calls his servants to comfort her. Whatever in the king's heart caused their thirty-day separation (cf. Esther 4:11) melts at the sight of Esther's fainting, and all is well again.

Of course, these examples are mere fables. They are not a part of God's inspired truth, a fact agreed upon by the majority of biblical scholars. These are "irreverent, silly myths" (1 Timothy 4:7) which "promote speculations rather than the stewardship from God that is by faith" (1 Timothy 1:4).

Any person who is overly interested in the "gaps" in God's Word or the mysteries of the faith is dangerous, especially if he is in the position of teacher. Don't mistake someone who knows a lot of trivia and fantasies for a good Bible teacher. He may lead you astray. There are many questions about the Bible that we will never be able to answer, simply because they are not a part of what God needs us to know for His grand purpose, which is to bring glory to His name (Isaiah 43:7). Moses said, "The secret things belong to the Lord our God, but the things that are revealed belong to us and to our children forever, that we may do all the words of this law" (Deuteronomy 29:29).

Equally dangerous is the teacher who has only an academic interest in the Bible. The Bible is meant to be lived and not just learned. Just because someone knows a lot of Bible trivia, that does not mean he should be leading a congregation of God's people. This is exactly the type of person Paul was warning Timothy about. Those who are strictly "academics," "intellectuals," or "storytellers" cause churches to lose their focus.

What is Paul's antidote to this distraction? In a word, *faith*. Timothy needed to be at Ephesus to fight this distraction because it promoted "speculations rather than the stewardship from God that is by faith."

Faith brings focus to the work of the Lord. In 1 Timothy 1, Paul emphasizes this by highlighting three goals that God has for His church. Without faith, a group of Christians can easily get away from these goals.

Stewardship

In verse 4, Paul expresses concern over those who have become distracted from the "stewardship from God that is by faith." The word translated "stewardship" (*oikonomia*) is notoriously difficult to render into English. Its generic meaning has to do with a household manager (cf. Luke 16:1-2). Here, the sense of a household may be retained, with the house being the church of God (1 Timothy 3:15; Ephesians 2:19; 1 Peter 2:5). William D. Mounce writes,

> Such an image is natural since the early church met in homes and referred to its members as "brother" and "sister." The idea is that Paul, the leaders of the churches, and all the members are to manage carefully the responsibilities and skills entrusted to them for the good of the others.[4]

Paul's faith made such a strong impression on him that he regarded his stewardship as an irresistible force (Ephesians 3:1-2; 1 Corinthians 9:16-17; Romans 1:14). In Paul's mind, preaching the gospel was not a choice that he had made so much as it was an obligation that had been laid upon him.

Paul Tillich defines faith as "ultimate concern." He goes on to say, "If [a concern] claims ultimacy it demands the total surrender of him who accepts this claim, and it promises total fulfillment even if all other claims have to be subjected to it or rejected in its name."[5] In other words, faith is concern for that which is most important, for God. When a person truly concerns himself with the Ultimate, no decisions have to be made about what comes first.

Everything – his family, his job, his money, even his basic necessities are subservient to the main focal point of his life – the Creator with Whom he expects to spend eternity.

Leaders of the church, and all Christians for that matter, have been entrusted with a stewardship of the gospel. Faith infuses that stewardship with a sense of obligation. It should feel as if we have no choice but to represent our Lord regardless of the sacrifice.

Love

Correcting the "swerving" direction of the distracted teachers, Paul reminds Timothy that "the aim of our charge is love that issues from a pure heart and a good conscience and a sincere faith" (v. 5). If you didn't catch it, Paul said that Christian love issues from three distinct sources.

A Pure Heart

Jesus called the pure in heart "blessed" (Matthew 5:8), and, like Paul, Peter encourages us to love one another earnestly from a pure heart (1 Peter 1:22).

We tend to isolate the heart to emotional territory, but biblically the heart has to do with thinking, feeling, and decision-making. A person's heart is his entire inner self. When the heart is "pure," it is undivided. No cracks compromise its integrity. A pure heart is essential to true love, since love is seeking the welfare of another over yourself.

A Good Conscience

Paul will later warn Timothy that soon some would depart from the faith "whose consciences are seared" (1 Timothy 4:2). Paul himself had always guarded his conscience, knowing how important it was to the life God had called him to live (Acts 23:1). This life includes, of course, the kind of love that Paul describes as the "aim" of his ministry.

A Sincere Faith

The pairing of faith and a good conscience is a recipe Paul will bring up again before the chapter is over (v. 19). Just as faith placed an obligation upon Paul to be a good steward of the gospel that had been entrusted to him, faith focused him on love. His understanding of the cross taught him how to love others (1 John 4:9-10).

Having briefly distinguished these three sources of Christian love, we can now combine them into one key condition that determines our capacity for love. Notice, all three adjectives have to do with uncompromised integrity: "pure," "good," and "sincere." Furthermore, the three nouns all have something to do with the inner self: "heart," "conscience," and "faith." Seeing this, we may summarize these three sources into one condition that will determine your capacity for love: *knowing yourself.*

Certainty about who you are, about your identity, was an obsession in Greek philosophy. Socrates said, "The unexamined life is not worth living." Another quote attributed to the Greeks reads, "Know thyself." This was good advice. A leading cause of hatred and strife is turmoil in the soul that comes from an inability or unwillingness to come to grips with who you are.

In "A Poison Tree," William Blake writes,

> I was angry with my friend;
> I told my wrath, my wrath did end.
> I was angry with my foe:
> I told it not, my wrath did grow.

And I waterd it in fears,
Night & morning with my tears:
and I sunned it with smiles,
and with soft deceitful wiles.

And it grew both day and night.
Till it bore an apple bright.
And my foe beheld it shine.
And he knew that it was mine.

And into my garden stole,
When the night had veild the pole;
In the morning glad I see;
My foe outstretched beneath the tree.

The protagonist was angry with both friend and foe. What made the difference in his relationship with the former and the latter? He told his wrath to his friend (he sought reconciliation), but when it came to his foe, he "told it not." He couldn't be honest with himself and open up to his enemy. That would have made him seem vulnerable (which he was), so instead, he nurtured his hatred into an apple, and at the end we see him smiling over his enemy's lifeless body.

 Your knowledge of yourself and of God's will for you decides your capacity for love. If you are insecure and unwilling to confess your true identity, you will be filled with hatred; you will not have much of a capacity to truly love in an open relationship. You will be afraid of the vulnerability and the risk of losing the relationship. However, if you understand that, like everyone else, you are a sinner who deserves death, but God loves you so much that He gave His only Son as a sacrifice and a substitute for your death, you will not be afraid of relationships because you know how solid the most important one is. And you will have a great capacity to love as God has loved you, because faith has taught you how.

Salvation

Paul now comes to the third goal on which his faith has focused him: "The saying is trustworthy and deserving of full acceptance, that Christ Jesus came into the world to save sinners, of whom I am the foremost" (v. 15).

Paul sees himself as an "example to those who were to believe in him for eternal life" (v. 16), and he was the very best example, because as the "foremost" of sinners, his salvation teaches all sinners the possibility of eternal life.

As painful as it is for him, Paul wants us to take a moment to reflect on different days, when he was known as "Saul of Tarsus." In those days he watched over the garments of the men who cruelly stoned Stephen the evangelist to death without cause (Acts 7:58). This same Saul was "breathing threats and murder against the disciples of the Lord" (Acts 9:1). He was a terrorist, going throughout Judea looking for those belonging to the Way, men or women, so that he could bring them in chains to Jerusalem (Acts 9:2). He confessed, "I persecuted this Way to the death, binding and delivering to prison both men and women" (Acts 22:4). How many men and women had he thrown into prison? How many children had he orphaned? How much blood had he spilled? The details are left up to our imaginations, but we know enough to stand with mouths agape at the sins of this man. And yet God not only forgave him, He appointed him to His service (1 Timothy 1:12).

How did Paul receive the promise of eternal life? He certainly did not earn it through good behavior. No, the "grace of our Lord overflowed" for him with the "faith and love that are in Christ Jesus" (1 Timothy 1:14). Faith and love led him to salvation in Jesus Christ. That same faith and love will take any person to the same place and leave him rejoicing over the promise of eternal life.

Like the early Christians in Ephesus, the church has lost its way. We live in a confusing world in which we have been divided over so many things. In every congregation where Christians meet, something is being taught, concerns are being shared, and leaders are leading the flock somewhere. The question is, has faith focused God's people in the right direction?

The aims that Paul shared with Timothy were clear and decisive:

- Don't neglect your stewardship of the house of God.
- Love one another from an undivided, uncompromising heart.
- Above all things, remember that Christ came to earth to save sinners. His mission is yours.

Faith will lift the fog of distraction from our churches and focus us so that vitality and growth will return to God's people. Faith is absolutely essential. Without it, we are utterly lost.

Discussion

1. Does your brand match your reputation? Does your reputation show that you have been able to stick to your goals?

2. Why would it be wrong to introduce a different doctrine from the one the apostles taught in the New Testament?

3. What did Paul mean when he warned Timothy about "myths and endless genealogies"?

4. Why should we be careful about teachers who like to share a lot of trivia and speculation about the Bible?

5. What was Paul's antidote to the distractions of different doctrines, myths, and endless genealogies?

6. What did Paul mean by the word "stewardship"?

7. Why did Paul regard preaching the gospel as an obligation?

8. What are the three sources of Christian love?

9. What is the key condition for love that surfaces when these three sources are combined?

10. How did Paul attain the promise of eternal life? Did he earn it? Or did he receive it in some other way?

TWO

FAITH WITHOUT GOD

"Man's nature, so to speak, is a perpetual factory of idols."
-John Calvin

Of course, it is possible to be lost, even with faith, if that faith is misdirected. Fearing this, James brings up the futility of faith without works and asks, "Can that faith save him?"[1] Apparently there is more than one kind of faith. James talked about faith without works and warns that it is "dead" (2:17). Jesus often rebuked His disciples' "little faith" (Matthew 6:30; 8:26; 14:31; 16:8) and commended a Gentile for his "great faith" (Matthew 8:10, KJV). In the last chapter, we mentioned Hymenaeus and Alexander who had "made shipwreck of their faith" (1 Timothy 1:19-20), and we could speak of other degrees of faith, some having the quality that saves, and some that are unacceptable in the eyes of God.

Because faith comes in different shapes and sizes, we will address forms of "primitive faith." Primitive faith is incomplete. In some cases, it is just getting started and is on its way to maturity. In other cases, it suffers from a dwarfism from which it will never recover. Faith that remains stunted and primitive cannot save, to answer James' question. Therefore, it must be identified and corrected.

While some see the benefits of faith, they do not want the spiritual baggage that comes with Christian faith, so they settle for something short of what God commands.

There are three particularly dangerous forms that we will discuss in this book: faith without God, faith without knowledge, and faith without works.

In this chapter, we will address the problem of faith without God. This is idolatrous faith, in which a person makes someone or something instead of God the object of his trust. Totem poles and golden idols have gone out of style in the part of the country where I live, so we rarely discuss the problem of idolatry. However, idolatry is a major theme in the Bible. It is not as though we have matured beyond the need for a discussion of these things; it is just that the idols have changed. Our idols are no longer made out of wood and stone but of subtler, and more dangerous, materials—ambition, money, power, ideology, and even flesh and blood.

I suppose humanity will never outgrow its penchant for worshiping idols. It is the nature of the human heart to replace God with counterfeits. Jeremiah, who knew our hearts, said, "The heart is deceitful above all things, and desperately sick; who can understand it?" (17:9). John Calvin memorably described our heartsickness by illustrating its fondness for substitutes for God: "Man's nature, so to speak, is a perpetual factory of idols."[2] Human beings are worshipful creatures. There has never been a society throughout civilization that has not been religious. So in the absence of any knowledge of God, people will find something or someone else to worship. G.K. Chesterton once observed, "When men cease to believe in God, they do not believe in nothing; they believe in anything."

This is a subject the writer of the book of Hebrews addressed with his audience of deserters who had been turning their back on faith in Christ. First, he recognized why faith is so attractive, and then he pointed out that when it is divorced from God, faith is utterly powerless.

The Lure of Faith

Why would somebody want faith without God? What makes faith so attractive, even when it's not connected to the true God? Faith is attractive because it is a transcendence of the soul. Skeptics have tried to deny God and criticize His Word, but they don't know what to do with qualities of the soul such as love, ambition, compassion, grief, worship, and artistic expression. Every person has been made in the image of God, and the soul is evidence of that. It's the soul that makes faith desirable to every human creature.

In Leo Tolstoy's *Anna Karenina*, the main character, Levin, finally comes to grips with his faith. He asks,

> Where could I have got it? By reason could I have arrived at knowing that I must love my neighbor and not oppress him? I was told that in my childhood, and I believed it gladly, *for they told me what was already in my soul.* But who discovered it? Not reason. Reason discovered the struggle for existence, and the law that requires us to oppress all who hinder the satisfaction of our desires. That is the deduction of reason. But loving one's neighbor reason could never discover, because it's irrational. (emphasis added)[3]

Jesus' teachings resonated with Levin because, as he said, they were "already in my soul." The lure of faith is its ability to touch us on the deepest level, in our soul.

Tolstoy's masterpiece was written before the Communists took over Russia and sought to eradicate faith in God from its people. For seventy years, the Russian people were in a spiritual captivity, forbidden from freely expressing their faith. Still, the longings of the soul could not be stamped out. After the Iron Curtain fell, religion flourished once more because the need for it had never been extinguished. Years ago, in a small village in southern Russia, I participated in an outdoor worship service with a small group of believers. While we were taking communion, I noticed how one of the sisters, almost in tears, brought the unleavened bread to her lips and kissed it before putting it into her mouth. I was struck by the tenderness and gratitude with which she observed what had been for me so many times a hollow ritual observed on the first day of every week. I was put to shame. Could it have been that this woman appreciated the Lord's Supper more than me because it had been forbidden for so long? I may not know the answer to this question, but I do know that the soul knows what it wants, and when it finds nourishment, the satisfaction is nothing short of exhilarating.

And souls are such fragile things. Without real faith in a real God, they wither away and leave us in an existential crisis. This is what the writer of Hebrews was trying to avoid when he wrote,

> Therefore do not throw away your confidence, which has a great reward. For you have need of endurance, so that when you have done the will of God you may receive what is promised. For, "Yet a little while, and the coming one will come and will not delay; but my righteous one shall live by faith, and if he shrinks back, my soul has no pleasure in him." But we are not of those who shrink back and are destroyed, but of

those who have faith and preserve their souls. Now faith is the assurance of things hoped for, the conviction of things not seen. (Hebrews 10:35-11:1)

"Do not throw away your confidence," he urges, "for you have need of endurance, so that when you have done the will of God you may receive what is promised." The Hebrews, no doubt, faced serious challenges that tempted them to turn their backs on Christ. Raymond Brown describes their situation:

> They had been physically assaulted, their homes had been plundered; some had been cast into prison on account of their faith, others had been ridiculed in public because of their resolute trust in Jesus. (10:32-34)[4]

It is understandable why some were "shrinking back," but this was destroying them. The writer was desperately urging them to hold onto their faith because faith would see them through these challenges to the "great reward" that God had "promised."

The biblical definition of faith is "the assurance of things hoped for, the conviction of things not seen" (11:1). Nobody is satisfied with things as they are. They either settle for a less than satisfying life, or they hope for something more. The fuel for this hope is faith. Faith is comforting because it builds an assurance that things will get better.

Faith is a very powerful force, and the world realizes this even if it doesn't believe in God. For this reason, faith has been hijacked by a world desiring transcendence without the spiritual baggage that comes with God.

But faith requires an object. That is where idols come in. Searching for transcendence, some have constructed idols to take the place of God.

Idolatrous Faith

After bringing up Enoch as an example of someone who was commended as having pleased God, the writer of Hebrews makes this statement: "And without faith it is impossible to please him, for whoever would draw near to God must believe that he exists and that he rewards those who seek him" (11:6). At first glance, here is what the writer appears to be saying: "Anybody who wants to have a relationship with God needs to do two things: 1) believe that He exists; and 2) believe that He rewards people who seek Him." But there is something wrong with this interpretation. Why would the writer tell someone who wants to be close to God that he first needs to believe in Him? Wouldn't a person who is trying to get to know God already believe in Him? There has to be something deeper at play here.

The verse makes more sense if we interpret "draw near" to refer to the kind of assurance and conviction faith brings according to verse 1. This interpretation is consistent with the writer's use of the phrase "draw near" throughout the book of Hebrews.

- In 4:16, it has to do with confidence in prayer, receiving mercy from God, and finding grace with Him.
- In 7:25, it has to do with being "saved to the uttermost" and knowing someone is interceding on your behalf.

- In 10:19-22, it has to do with confidence, having a true heart, a clean conscience, and full assurance of faith.

A better interpretation, then, would be: "Whoever desires confidence and freedom from self-doubt and feelings of acceptance must first believe that God exists and also believe that He rewards those who have this faith." This interpretation requires faith in the right object. It is not enough to simply "believe." What you believe in is just as important as the belief itself.

This is why idolatrous faith is so destructive. When you trust in the wrong thing, you do not get the same results as you would if you were trusting in God.

Today's idols are just as destructive as Baal and Molech, even more so because they are not as obvious. Regardless of the shape or form an idol comes in, idolatry will eventually lead you to condemnation because it asks you to put your faith in someone or something other than God.

Science

The strange but commonplace worship of science makes it one of the most dangerous idols in society. Richard Dawkins, a professor at Oxford University, says that with the advent of Darwin's theory of evolution, "it is possible to be an intellectually fulfilled atheist."[5] Stephen Edelglass, Georg Maier, Hans Gebert, and John Davy in their book, *The Marriage of Sense and Thought*, wrote that "Science now functions in society rather as the church did in the Middle Ages."[6] Wendell Berry writes,

> the religification and evangelizing of science, in defiance of scientific principles, is now commonplace

and is widely accepted or tolerated by people who are not scientists. We really seem to have conceded to scientists, to the extent of their own regrettable willingness to occupy it, the place once occupied by the prophets and priests of religion.[7]

Part of science's appeal is the illusion that through science we will one day understand everything there is to know about our universe. Mystery and limited intelligence are frowned upon as failures of humanity. This perception puts God at odds with science, which is a fairly recent development. Even Einstein admitted: "Science without religion is lame; religion without science is blind."[8] But instead of looking at faith in God as the perfect complement to science, many modern scientists cast it off as hokum and believe that if there are any answers, they can only be found in science. They are like Dr. Kelvin in Andrei Tarkovsky's *Solaris* (1972) whose colleague argued, "You want to destroy what you don't understand. Knowledge is beautiful only if it's based on morality."

Science is helpful only if we can understand its limitations. Science is not meant to deal with all the realities, just those that can be subjected to the scientific method, which requires experimenting with empirical evidence (i.e., that which can be detected by the five senses). Realities beyond the empirical must be discovered without science. These are realities concerning the big questions: Where did I come from? Why am I here? Where am I going?

Humanity
"Cursed is the man who trusts in man and makes flesh his strength, whose heart turns away from the Lord" (Jeremiah

17:5). These are the words of the prophet Jeremiah, uttered during the time when God had been forgotten and humankind had centered the universe upon itself. What are the results of faith in humanity? "[The man who trusts in man] is like a shrub in the desert, and shall not see any good come. He shall dwell in the parched places of the wilderness, in an uninhabited salt land" (v. 6). On the other hand, the man who trusts in the Lord "is like a tree planted by water, that sends out its roots by the stream, and does not fear when he comes, for its leaves remain green, and is not anxious in the year of drought, for it does not cease to bear fruit" (v. 8).

Faith in humanity over God has two subdivisions. First, there is the faith that one person has in another. Maybe a person trusts in the president or his father or some church leader. Regardless of the talents and intelligence of the one in whom the trust is given, eventually the believer's hopes will be crushed. No one on earth can take the place of God.

The other subdivision of this type of faith is trust in oneself. When a person's faith is centered on himself, his will comes before everyone else's. He is selfish and cannot truly love or cultivate solid relationships. There are actually several subdivisions within this one. The worship of sex, power, and money are all simply manifestations of worshiping oneself. Even self-righteousness falls into this category. Think of the Pharisee in Luke 18 who prayed, "God, I thank you that I am not like other men, extortioners, unjust, adulterers, or even like this tax collector. I fast twice a week; I give tithes of all that I get" (v. 12). Luke describes the Pharisee as "standing by himself," or, as some translations render it, he "prayed thus with himself" (v. 11, NKJV). Either way the meaning is essentially the same. If he was praying with himself he was praying by himself. In other words, he had made himself, not God, the point of his prayer.

Images of God
The second commandment given to Moses on Sinai read,

> You shall not make for yourself a carved image, or any likeness of anything that is in heaven above, or that is in the earth beneath, or that is in the water under the earth. You shall not bow down to them or serve them, for I the Lord your God am a jealous God, visiting the iniquity of the fathers on the children to the third and the fourth generation of those who hate me, but showing steadfast love to thousands of those who love me and keep my commandments. (Exodus 20:4-6)

Moses reminded Israel of this commandment as they stood on the banks of the Jordan preparing to enter into the Promised Land:

> Therefore watch yourselves very carefully. Since you saw no form on the day that the Lord spoke to you at Horeb out of the midst of the fire, beware lest you act corruptly by making a carved image for yourselves, in the form of any figure, the likeness of male or female, the likeness of any animal that is on the earth, the likeness of any winged bird that flies in the air, the likeness of anything that creeps on the ground, the likeness of any fish that is in the water under the earth. And beware lest you raise your eyes to heaven, and when you see the sun and the moon and the stars, all the host of heaven, you be drawn away and bow down to them and serve them, things that the Lord

your God has allotted to all the peoples under the whole heaven. (Deuteronomy 4:15-18)

Why was God so explicit in His instructions about making images? Why did He command the Israelites to "watch yourselves very carefully"? Students of the history of Israel from the Old Testament know that the downfall of Israel was idols of this sort, images made of stone and wood. What was wrong with images to aid their worship? What if a visual idea of God assisted their devotion to Him? We have religious groups today that use icons and images in their Christian worship. Are they wrong?

God's forceful prohibition against images was given in part because these idols conveyed false ideas about Him.[9] How can you conceptualize the invisible, infinite God? You simply can't. If you try, your inadequate picture of the One whom you are worshiping eventually comes to represent Him, and before you know it, you're not worshiping God, but an inadequate representation of God. John warned, "No one has ever seen God" (John 1:18), and Paul exclaimed, "How unsearchable are his judgments and how inscrutable his ways!" (Romans 11:33). Some people say, "I like to think of Him as a grandfather," or they talk about "the man upstairs." God has made us in His image. Beware of trying to make Him in yours! He is a jealous God and will not share His glory with another (Isaiah 48:11).

The plea of Hebrews 11:6 is for a faith that knows God as He wants to be known. Jesus' mission on earth was to supply our faith with the proper object. The Lord told Philip, "Whoever has seen me has seen the Father" (John 14:9). Faith without God will not support a soul that longs for transcendence. Faith in any god, too, will lead to crushing disappointment. Only faith in the God of the

Bible, that God Jesus revealed when He came to earth, will sustain us against the hard struggles of life.

Discussion

1. Give some examples of the different forms of faith.

2. What is primitive faith?

3. Is it still important to talk about idolatry? In what ways has idolatry changed?

4. Why is faith attractive? Why is it desirable to every human creature?

5. What is the definition of faith according to Hebrews 11:1?

6. What does the phrase "draw near" mean in the context of the book of Hebrews?

7. Why are so many drawn to science as a substitute for God?

8. Does science have limitations? What are they?

9. What are the two subdivisions of faith in humanity?

10. What is wrong with images of God?

11. How may we come to know the God of the Bible and put our faith in Him?

THREE

FAITH WITHOUT KNOWLEDGE

"For I bear them witness that they have a zeal for God, but not according to knowledge."

-Romans 10:2

While the powerful lure of faith has tempted some to replace God so they can do away with the spiritual baggage that goes along with Him, it has tempted others to put the cart before the horse so to speak and take the "leap of faith" that so many religious people praise and so many atheists criticize.

Blind, unquestioning conviction is the common perception of what Christian faith is supposed to be. Many atheists have pointed this out to discredit Christianity. Richard Robinson wrote that Christian faith is

> believing that there is a God no matter what the evidence on the question may be. "Have faith," in the Christian sense, means "make yourself believe that there is a god without regard to evidence." Christian faith is a habit of flouting reason in forming and maintaining one's answer to the question whether there is a god.[1]

In more recent times, Sam Harris wrote: "In fact, every religion preaches the truth of propositions for which no evidence is even *conceivable*." Richard Dawkins in *The God Delusion* said: "The whole point of religious faith, its strength and chief glory, is that it does not depend on rational justification."[3]

Sadly, the skeptics are not so much battling a strawman as they are attacking the prevailing religious view of faith, which is a faith without knowledge. *Webster's New World College Dictionary* defines faith as "unquestioning belief that does not require proof or evidence." Also, the Christian mystic, Khalil Gibran said, "Faith is a knowledge within the heart, beyond the reach of proof." And the popular Christian psychologist James Dobson wrote, "Matters of faith can never be proved; they always have to be 'the substance of things hoped for, the evidence of things not seen' (Hebrews 11:1, KJV)."[4] The common view of faith, even among religious people, is that faith steps into the dark pools of ignorance where knowledge dares not encroach. Faith supplies us with the strength, joy, and the guidance we need when God is silent and there is no proof or factual basis for our lives. "Just have faith" is the mantra that drives most religious actions.

Dobson's statement brings up the point that numerous biblical texts appear to support this view of faith. He believes the phrase "things not seen" in Hebrews 11:1 means absolutely no evidence whatsoever is required for faith. Another frequently quoted passage is 2 Corinthians 5:7: "For we walk by faith, not by sight." Purveyors of blind faith also champion Thomas, who was asked, "Have you believed because you have seen me? Blessed are those who have not seen and yet have believed" (Jn. 20:29). It is true that some verses say our faith is not based on what we see with our eyes, but they say nothing about "blind faith," that is, faith without evidence. They do not rule out all lines of evidence, just "sight." "Sight" is the biblical way of speaking of empirical evidence (proofs that can only be discovered by the five senses). Just because we cannot know that God exists through "sight," that does not mean we cannot discover Him by other types of evidence. For example, after John relates Jesus' statement to Thomas, he writes:

> Now Jesus did many other signs in the presence of the disciples, which are not written in this book; but these are written so that you may believe that Jesus is the Christ, the Son of God, and that by believing you may have life in his name. (John 20:30-31)

John followed Jesus' blessing upon those who believe in Him without "seeing" with an explanation that his gospel account was written to produce saving faith. John's gospel does not fit within the category of "things seen," but it is evidence that can lead to faith.

What about this evidence? The pursuit of faith can be very frustrating when this evidence is not apparent. In Ingmar Bergman's film *The Seventh Seal* (1957), a knight named Antonius Block returns from the Crusades crushed and doubting the religious beliefs he had held his entire life. In a confession booth he asks, "Is it so terribly inconceivable to comprehend God with one's senses? Why does He hide in a cloud of half-promises and unseen miracles? …Why is He, despite all, a mocking reality I can't be rid of?" Block becomes so desperate that he accosts a young woman accused of practicing witchcraft on her way to the burning pyre on which she is to be executed: "They say you have consorted with the devil?" The witch replies, "Why do you ask that?" "It's not out of curiosity," Block says, "but because of utterly personal reasons. I would also like to meet him."

"Why?" she asks. The knight says, "I want to ask him about God. He must know. He, if anyone."

It is not necessary to live in the spiritual anguish exhibited by Bergman's troubled knight. In the book of Romans, Paul speaks of three lines of evidence that bring knowledge to our faith. While each of these is compelling on its own, it is important for the believer to learn all three in order to develop true, biblical faith.

The Existence of God

In the last chapter, we noted Hebrews 11:6, which says that whoever would draw near to God "must believe that he exists and that he rewards those who seek him." But is it really possible for someone to believe in God because of evidence outside of the Bible?

Paul thought so. The book of Romans begins with an argument that all have sinned and fall short of the glory of God (Romans 3:23). Paul builds up to this conclusion by first indicting the Gentiles of sin and then turning to the Jews. But he faces a challenge when confronting the Gentiles. What if they try to get off the hook by pointing out that the law was never given to them? They could argue that "apart from the law, sin lies dead" (Romans 7:8); since they never heard Moses' legislation, it would be wrong for them to be held accountable to it. Paul doesn't claim they should be held accountable to the law of Moses, but he does stick with his point that they have sinned and are in need of a Savior. Instead of pointing to God's special revelation, His written Word, he calls to the witness stand the obvious marks the Creator left on the world He had designed:

> For the wrath of God is revealed from heaven against all ungodliness and unrighteousness of men, who by

their unrighteousness suppress the truth. For what can be known about God is plain to them, because God has shown it to them. For his invisible attributes, namely, his eternal power and divine nature, have been clearly perceived, ever since the creation of the world, in the things that have been made. So they are without excuse. (Romans 1:18-20)

Perhaps the apostle was thinking of the Psalms where the same argument can be found: "The heavens declare the glory of God, and the sky above proclaims his handiwork. Day to day pours out speech, and night to night reveals knowledge" (Psalm 19:1-2). David, who had spent many nights outdoors when he was a shepherd, often slept under the night sky and wondered at its beauty and intricate design. How could all of this have just happened? Surely a magnificent Creator made it!

This evidence may not reveal specific information about sin, redemption, the church, morality, and the afterlife, but at the very least it puts knowledge of the existence of God into our heart. We may not know much about His moral characteristics—our knowledge may be limited to his "eternal power and divine nature"—but it is a start. Faith cannot be conceived, however, without more information.

Morality

I have already mentioned Leo Tolstoy's book *Anna Karenina* in which a character named Levin develops Christian faith. Levin reflects some of Tolstoy's own spiritual journey from agnosticism to belief in God. Tolstoy's apologetics are revealed through the thin screen of one of Levin's soliloquies:

...we are all agreed about this one thing: what we must live for and what is good. I and all men have only one firm, incontestable, clear knowledge, and that knowledge cannot be explained by the reason—it is outside it, and has no causes and can have no effects.

If goodness has causes, it is not goodness; if it has effects, a reward, it is not goodness either. So goodness is outside the chain of cause and effect.

And yet I know it, and we all know it.

What could be a greater miracle than that?[5]

At first, it may appear that Levin is taking a leap of faith, but there is more to his belief than a leap into the unknown. Levin has a firm conviction in the concept of "goodness," but he doesn't know where he got this idea if it did not come from God. He knows that if there is a cause, or motive, behind goodness, it is not really goodness; it is merely an effort to gain something by manipulation. Furthermore, goodness has no effects, or rewards, because, again, if there is a reward, your goodwill is self-interest rather than altruism. If goodness has no cause or effect, it must have been planted in us by God. What alternative do we have? Evolution? No, the mechanism behind evolution is natural selection, survival of the fittest, which is on the opposite end of the spectrum from benevolence. Goodness comes from heavenly realms.

This is yet another line of evidence found in the book of Romans. Still speaking of the Gentiles, Paul writes,

> For when Gentiles, who do not have the law, by nature do what the law requires, they are a law to

themselves, even though they do not have the law. They show that the work of the law is written on their hearts, while their conscience also bears witness, and their conflicting thoughts accuse or even excuse them. (Romans 2:14-15)

The Gentiles did not have a law like the one given to the Jews from Mount Sinai, yet "by nature" they did what the law required. In other words, they knew instinctively what the Ten Commandments declared: that one should honor his mother and father, that it is wrong to murder, that it is wrong to commit adultery, that it is wrong to steal, that it is wrong to bear false witness against your neighbor, and that it is wrong to covet your neighbor's house. Why is it that even without a law given from heaven, it is in the wiring of humanity to observe these fundamental rules of morality? Why do people feel guilty about violating Christian principles, even if they have never been exposed Christianity? How do you explain the universal existence of the human conscience?

This morality is broken down into three areas by the apostle Paul. First, he speaks of "the work of the law...written on their hearts." He speaks of moral obligation, what C.S. Lewis referred to as "a real law which we did not invent and which we know we ought to obey."[6] One cannot deny that it is human nature to observe this law. An obvious historical example is the Nuremberg trials in which the Nazis were accused of cruel and murderous treatment of the Jewish race. Their defense was that their society had its own needs and desires and had made its own laws. These laws dictated to them the extermination of the Jews. According to the accused Nazis, it would have been wrong for them to break the laws of their society. Their point was that their prosecutors were trying them by the laws of an alien society. What if they had been tried by a court that believed mankind was nothing more than a cosmic accident resulting from billions of years of evolutionary progress? That court could not have appealed to any law higher than that of each individual society, and the Nazis would have been justified by their case. They simply obeyed the laws of their own society. They were not excused, however. They were found guilty by a higher law, which according to the prosecutor, Robert Jackson, in his closing address, "rises above the provincial and transient." To what higher law did Jackson appeal? Was it not the moral law God created in humanity, the law written on our hearts?[7]

The second area recognized by Paul is the "conscience" that was bearing witness against the Gentiles. The conscience is an urge that tells us what we ought or ought not to do. Coupled with the law written on our hearts, it bears witness as in a trial, urging us to do what is right. However, the conscience is merely an urge to do what has been programmed into our intellects, and this creates the possibility of following the conscience and still disobeying God. Paul is the perfect example. On trial before the Sanhedrin, he said, "I have lived my life before God in all good conscience up to this day" (Acts 23:1). We know that Paul committed grievous sins before he became a Christian, imprisoning Christians and even putting some of them to death. Evidently, he was following his conscience when he did this, but his intellect had been programmed by his pharisaical upbringing to commit these hideous acts of terrorism. That is why the Word of God is so important. Without it, the conscience is handicapped and will not always lead us in the right direction.

The third and final area mentioned by Paul are the "thoughts" that "accuse or even excuse" the Gentiles. We call this the gift of common sense. When faced with tough moral decisions and questions about the will of God, we must think with common sense in the exercise of our volition to do the right thing.

Morality, despite its universal presence, will not by itself ensure that a person has enough knowledge to believe in the true God, but it is an important part of the knowledge base needed for proper faith. There is yet one more piece to the puzzle.

The Word of God
By the time we get to Romans 10, Paul is no longer dealing with the Gentiles. He is now arguing with Jews who will not accept the Gentiles as fellow believers and who will not accept the gospel's system of salvation by faith instead of by works of the law. They have a "zeal for God," says Paul, "but not according to knowledge" (v. 2). The Word of God has plainly declared that salvation is possible for whomever calls on the name of the Lord (vv. 11, 13). But it appears that many of Paul's enemies have not been studying their Bibles. So Paul traces faith backwards to its source for them in an effort to explain the importance of coupling faith and zeal with knowledge:

> How then will they call on him in whom they have not believed? And how are they to believe in him of whom they have never heard? And how are they to hear without someone preaching? And how are they to preach unless they are sent? As it is written, "How beautiful are the feet of those who preach the good news!" But they have not all obeyed the gospel. For

Isaiah says, "Lord, who has believed what he has heard from us?" So faith comes from hearing, and hearing through the word of Christ. (Romans 10:14 – 17)

The third and final part of knowledge has now been set in place. With a firm belief in the existence of the Creator, and the divine moral law written on the heart, an understanding of the Word of God will produce the faith that God desires. "Faith comes from hearing, and hearing through the word of Christ." In the prayer Jesus uttered on the eve of His arrest, He anticipated this kind of faith, praying for those who would believe in Him through the word of His disciples (John 17:20). Peter and the others fulfilled their Lord's wishes so that "the Gentiles should hear the word of the gospel and believe" (Acts 15:7). Without the knowledge that comes from God's Word, faith cannot be fully conceived, only partially developed.

In *Robinson Crusoe*, the main character spies a footprint in the sand that is clearly not his own. From the presence of this footprint, he concludes that someone else is on the island. Over the course of time, he discovers that the footprint belongs to a man he names "Friday." What if he had never found Friday? In other words, what if he had never been able to see the man with his eyes or feel him with his hands? What if he had never heard the sound of his voice? Would that have made Friday's existence any less plain to him? After some time of looking for him unsuccessfully, Crusoe might have had his doubts, but his thoughts would have always returned to that footprint. The only explanation for that footprint was that a man had shared his island with him for a period of time, even if he was no longer there.[8]

God has left footprints, three in particular: the marks of His design in the world He created; the law of morality written on our hearts; and His inspired Word that is infallible and free from errors. The presence of these three indelible footprints means that believing in Jesus Christ is not a leap into the darkness, but a rational response to a God who wants to save us.

Discussion

1. What is "blind faith"? Is this a biblical faith?

2. What do you think about *Webster's* definition of faith as "unquestioning belief that does not require proof or evidence"?

3. Can we believe in God because of evidence other than that which can be seen by the eyes?

4. What are some of the verses used in support of blind faith? Discuss how these verses should be interpreted.

5. How does nature testify to the existence of God?

6. How does goodness and morality testify to the Creator?

7. Can morality be explained by reason or science? If not, where does morality come from?

8. Give the three areas into which morality is broken down by Paul in Romans 2:14-15.

9. Why is the Word of God so important to the knowledge that should accompany faith?

10. What "footprints" has God left to give us reasons to believe in Him?

FOUR

FAITH WITHOUT WORKS

"For faith is only real when there is obedience, never without it, and faith only becomes faith in the act of obedience."

-Dietrich Bonhoeffer

How far should the rational response of faith go? Is saving faith simply an acceptance of the facts? ("I know that I should.") Or does it go deeper to the level of trust? ("I will *do* what I know that I should.")

Let's say I go to my father and ask him how to handle a problem I am having with a friend. He says, "If you really want to save your friendship, go to him and say you are sorry, and he will forgive you. Trust me." I could respond on two different levels. On one level, I could think, "I know that he is right, but I cannot bring myself to go to my friend and say that I am sorry." I agree in my heart with my father, but I do not trust him enough to follow through with his advice. On another level, I could actually do what he suggested. This is trust.

The question before us is: does the faith that justifies sinners look like the first level of agreeing with my father's advice but doing nothing, or does it look like the second level of trusting my father enough to follow his advice? The doctrine of justification by faith alone thinks of faith in terms of the first level. As John Piper said, "Godly works do not begin to have a role in our lives until we are justified.

We are declared righteous by faith alone while we are still ungodly."[1]

To clarify, there is no question that God justifies sinners by faith. The New Testament makes this very plain. In Romans, Paul writes,

> Now to the one who works, his wages are not counted as a gift but as his due. And to the one who does not work but believes in him who justifies the ungodly, his faith is counted as righteousness. (Romans 4:4-5)

To the Galatians he wrote,

> Yet we know that a person is not justified by works of the law but through faith in Jesus Christ, so we also have believed in Christ Jesus, in order to be justified by faith in Christ and not by works of the law, because by works of the law no one will be justified. (Galatians 2:16)

His thoughts remain consistent in Ephesians: "For by grace you have been saved through faith. And this is not your own doing; it is the gift of God, not a result of works, so that no one may boast" (Ephesians 2:8-9).

The question we are wrestling with has to do with the *nature* of the faith that justifies. Is it interior, or does it express itself in obedience?

Martin Luther

During the Middle Ages, the Roman Catholic Church turned Christian faith into a to-do list of rituals and prayers that, if successfully performed, supposedly granted the worshiper access into God's good graces. The works-based salvation promoted by Catholicism looked very similar to the religion of the Pharisees that Jesus so passionately rebuked. Sinners desperate for God's mercy turned to their priests for guidance, only to receive a prescription for a certain number of prayers, deeds of penance, or even taxation. These duties left the soul thirsting for more, as they did nothing to assure sinners that their sins had been forgiven. The works they had been given to do only added to their guilt by giving them more righteous deeds they would not be able to complete to perfection.

One German monk who belonged to this mass of agonizing sinners was Martin Luther. Luther entered a monastery in Erfurt, Germany, in 1505 where he gained recognition for his keen intellect. By 1512 he was teaching as a professor of theology at the University in Wittenberg, Germany.[2] Despite his religious fervor and the recognition he received from the church, Luther could not find peace. Looking back on those days, he wrote,

> Though I lived as a monk without reproach, I felt that I was a sinner before God with an extremely disturbed conscience. I cannot believe that he was placated by my satisfaction. I did not love, yes, I hated the righteous God who punishes sinners, and secretly, if not blasphemously, certainly murmuring greatly, I was angry with God, and said, "As if, indeed, it is not enough, that miserable sinners, eternally lost through original sin, are crushed by every kind of calamity by the law of the decalogue, without having God add pain to pain by the gospel and also by the gospel threatening us with his righteous wrath!" Thus I raged with a fierce and troubled conscience.[3]

Moved by this restlessness, Luther lectured on the Psalms and the book of Romans and through these studies came to a conclusion that would revolutionize theology: *God justifies man freely by faith, not by any work of merit that he can do.* This insight became the basis of Luther's understanding of the gospel. He wrote, "This doctrine is the head and the cornerstone. It alone begets, nourishes, builds, preserves, and defends the church of God; and without it the church of God cannot exist for one hour."[4]

Convinced that this idea would gain traction with the church in Rome, Luther famously nailed a document called the "Ninety-Five Theses" to the door of the cathedral in Wittenberg to challenge the Pope and his priests on this and other controversial aspects of Catholicism. Unfortunately, the two sides were never able to reconcile, and Christianity splintered into thousands of denominations.

Conditions for Salvation

While Luther's doctrine puts the responsibility for salvation squarely on the shoulders of the only one who is willing and able to give it – God – it fails to clarify the meaning of the "faith" that saves and the "works" that cannot justify the sinner according to Paul. Does the New Testament teach that a person can have saving faith without obeying the Word? Furthermore, do all works fall into the category of the kind of deeds that stand opposed to faith in justification? If so, how should we read conditions for salvation in the New Testament, such as:

> No, I tell you; but unless you repent, you will all likewise perish. (Luke 13:3)

> Because, if you confess with your mouth that Jesus is Lord and believe in your heart that God raised him from the dead, you will be saved. For with the heart one believes and is justified, and with the mouth one confesses and is saved. (Romans 10:9-10)
>
> Whoever believes and is baptized will be saved, but whoever does not believe will be condemned. (Mark 16:16)
>
> Repent and be baptized every one of you in the name of Jesus Christ for the forgiveness of your sins, and you will receive the gift of the Holy Spirit. (Acts 2:38)
>
> And now why do you wait? Rise and be baptized and wash away your sins, calling on his name. (Acts 22:16)

These verses and many more teach that God requires certain conditions to be met before He will forgive a believer's sins. Unless a person trusts Him enough to repent, confess, and be baptized, he will not "be saved" and have his sins washed away.

The problem with Luther's doctrine is that it interferes with these plain biblical commands. Because of its oversimplification of "faith" and "works," this teaching moves talented writers and preachers to deny the importance of baptism in God's plan of salvation. Take, for example, this statement by Stan Norman: "Although insisting that baptism is unnecessary for salvation, Baptists contend that it is important and necessary for church membership."[5] Also, consider this statement by Donna Ascol: "I am convinced by Scripture that only those who are saved by God's grace are scriptural candidates for baptism." Even though she says she has arrived at this conclusion through the study of "Scripture," she quotes only from Romans 6:4, a passage that teaches that "newness of life" does not precede but *follows* baptism![6]

Faulty applications from Luther's doctrine of justification by faith alone have even made their way into the backs of editions of the Bible. One publication of the English Standard Version contains a section in the back entitled "God's Plan to Save You." Here is how it instructs its readers to be justified by faith:

> You may express your faith in Him by praying this prayer: Heavenly Father, I believe that Jesus Christ is your Son, and that He died on the cross to save me from my sin. I believe that He rose again to life, and that He invites me to live forever with Him in heaven as a part of your family. Because of what Jesus has done, I ask You to forgive me of my sin and give me eternal life. I invite You to come into my heart and life. I want to trust Jesus as my Savior and follow Him as my Lord. Help me to live in a way that pleases and honors You. Amen.[7]

According to this guide, all one needs to do in order to believe "in" God is pray a version of what is commonly called the "Sinner's Prayer" (a "work"). Beyond this, the amount of obedience required of a person of faith for salvation is up to him.

Faith Without Works Is Dead
While Luther took great comfort in the writings of the apostle Paul, he did not know what to do with the epistle of James. He was so troubled by James' statement that "faith

by itself, if it does not have works, is dead" (James 2:17) that he questioned whether it belonged in the New Testament, calling it an "epistle of straw."

James does present a problem for those who teach salvation by faith alone. In James 2:14-26, we find three main clauses that confront this teaching:

- "So also faith by itself, if it does not have works, is dead" (v. 17).
- "... faith apart from works is useless ("dead," KJV)..." (v. 20).
- "For as the body apart from the spirit is dead, so also faith apart from works is dead" (v. 26).

Fundamentally, James sees death as a separation. The physical death of a person involves the separation of his body from the spirit. So what would you call faith separated from works? Is it not a "dead" faith?

James describes works as the lifeblood of faith. Why is it so important for a believer to act on his faith? James gives three reasons.

Faith without Works Is a Problem

"What good is it," James asks, "my brothers, if someone says he has faith but does not have works? Can that faith save him?" (v. 14). Does James contradict the passages from Paul's letters cited above? No, James and Paul may have different emphases, but they are not at odds with one another. Paul had to deal with an audience that was trying to earn its way into heaven, while James battled the problem of a lifeless faith that produced nothing. Paul and James actually complement one another.

The lifelessness of this faith shows in the example James gives: "If a brother or sister is poorly clothed and lacking in daily food, and one of you says to them, 'Go in peace, be warmed and filled,' without giving them the things needed for the body, what good is that?" (vv. 15-16). This is a faith that results in "words" but not "works." Imagine that someone from your congregation lost her home in a fire. All of her worldly goods vanished in a cloud of smoke. And when you see her on Sunday, you do nothing but walk by, pat her on the shoulder, and say, "Too bad. Our prayers are with you." You don't even really bother to pray for her. It would have been better to do nothing. Empty words demonstrate nothing in the way of faith, which leads us to James' second reason why it is so important for faith to be accompanied by works.

Faith without Works Cannot Be Proven
James continues his argument, posing a slightly different scenario: "But someone will say, 'You have faith and I have works.' Show me your faith apart from your works, and I will show you my faith by my works" (v. 18). He imagines another person who is arguing with him and says, "One person has faith, and another has works. A person's devotion to God is not always exhibited in the same fashion. I might show my loyalty to God by faith, while another person may show it by works, but each is equally valid."

James answers this objection in two ways. Regarding the first case, the person who shows his devotion to God through faith only, he says, "Show me your faith apart from your works." Of course, this is impossible. Faith is invisible. It can only be detected by the actions it produces. Regarding the second case, the person who has works, he says, "I will show you my faith by my works." In other words, "I will *prove* my faith by works." When James is finished with this imaginary objector, one point is clear: faith without works cannot be proven.

In the last chapter we saw that knowledge precedes faith. Now it is becoming clear that faith precedes works. Some try to stop faith before it produces its natural fruit. To these, James says, "You foolish person, faith apart from works is useless" (v. 20). Others skip faith so that they can get a head start on works. This is just as bad as faith alone. When a person has no faith, his obedience turns legalistic and ugly.

James points out that even the demons believe – and shudder!" (v. 19). The demons believed that there was one God (James 2:19), that Jesus was divine (Mark 3:11-12), that there was a place of eternal punishment (Luke 8:30-31), and that Jesus was their judge (Mark 5:1-13). What was the outcome of their belief? Shuddering! Faith without works is a kind of faith, the faith of demons – a useless, powerless faith that leads to nothing but sheer terror.

Faith without Works Cannot Be Perfected
We have been discussing examples of primitive faith: faith without God, faith without knowledge, and now faith without works. This is faith that is incomplete. Some of the saddest examples in the Bible pertain to people with incomplete faith. On one occasion, Jesus perceived that a scribe had answered Him wisely and said, "You are not far from the kingdom of God" (Mark 12:34). Someone might take this as a compliment, but Jesus did not say this man was in the kingdom, just that he was "not far." If that man remained in this condition on Judgment Day, "not far" would not do him much good. If he is "not far" from the kingdom on that day, he might as well be a million miles

away. In another example, Jesus discussed eternal life with a rich young ruler and had to say, "One thing you still lack" (Luke 18:22). The story ends by describing the young man as "very sad" (v. 23). When Paul gave his defense before King Agrippa in Caesarea, he confronted the ruler, boldly saying, "I know that you believe." Evidently, Agrippa's belief had not grown to include trust, for he said, "You almost persuade me to become a Christian" (Acts 26:28, NKJV). The king's incomplete faith inspired the refrain, "Almost persuaded... Almost but lost!"

Faith, if it is going to save, must be perfected. To illustrate, James reminds his readers of two important examples from the Old Testament. He first recalls the Father of the Faithful:

> Was not Abraham our father justified by works when he offered up his son Isaac on the altar? You see that faith was active along with his works, and faith was completed by his works; and the Scripture was fulfilled that says, "Abraham believed God, and it was counted to him as righteousness"—and he was called a friend of God. You see that a person is justified by works and not by faith alone. (vv. 21-24)

Abraham already believed that God existed and that He followed through with His promises when God commanded him to do the unthinkable and offer his only son Isaac as a burnt offering on the mountains of Moriah. According to what James writes, Abraham was not justified when he went to bed that evening determined to follow through with the Lord's request. His consideration that God might raise his son from the dead was not even enough (cf. Hebrews 11:19). Nor was he justified when he rose early the next morning, saddled his donkey, summoned Isaac, and cut the wood for the burnt offering. It wasn't until he was in the act of following through with this gruesome deed that God stopped him and said, "Now I know that you fear God, seeing you have not withheld your son, your only son from me" (Genesis 22:12). God promised to bless him and reiterated the covenant made with him before "because you have obeyed my voice" (Genesis 22:18).

The only passage James quotes precedes the event of Abraham's sacrifice by many years: "Abraham believed God, and it was counted to him as righteousness" (Genesis 15:6). If God had counted his faith as righteousness long before Isaac was even born, how can James' argument be explained? Faith doesn't form instantly; it develops over time. This has hopefully been apparent as we have been discussing primitive faith in terms of first matching faith with the proper God and then linking it with knowledge of His divine nature and eternal power, notions of right and wrong, and God's Word. Faith in its maturity expresses itself through obedience. God knew before Isaac was born that Abraham's faith was real, so before his faith yielded the ultimate obedience, God counted it as righteousness.

James gives us another example of an individual who believed in a merciful God and expressed this belief through obedience: "And in the same way was not also Rahab the prostitute justified by works when she received the messengers and sent them out by another way?" (v. 25). Everyone in Jericho had the same intelligence as Rahab about the miracle of the Red Sea and the Israelites' victories over the kings in the east. But only Rahab expressed her faith to the spies and "sent them out by another way." Joshua 2 records that she confessed,

I know that the Lord has given you the land, and that the fear of you has fallen upon us, and that all the inhabitants of the land melt away before you. For we have heard how the Lord dried up the water of the Red Sea before you when you came out of Egypt, and what you did to the two kings of the Amorites who were beyond the Jordan, to Sihon and Og, whom you devoted to destruction. And as soon as we heard it, our hearts melted, and there was no spirit left in any man because of you, for the Lord your God, he is God in the heavens above and on the earth beneath. Now then, please swear to me by the Lord that, as I have dealt kindly with you, you also will deal kindly with my father's house, and give me a sure sign that you will save alive my father and mother, my brothers and sisters, and all who belong to them, and deliver our lives from death. (Joshua 2:8-13)

For Abraham, perfect faith involved obeying a crushing command from God regarding his son. For Rahab, it involved turning her back on her own people to help the Israelite spies. What does trusting Jesus involve for us? Certainly it involves looking after those who cannot stand up for themselves. This is the specific kind of obedience James is addressing when he talks about faith and works in James 2. In 1:27 he describes pure and undefiled religion in terms of visiting orphans and widows in their affliction and keeping oneself unstained from the world. Chapter 2 begins with a condemnation of showing partiality and reaches its climax with a rebuke of the kind of faith that will not even put clothes on someone's back and food in his belly.

Does perfect faith not also require obedience to the moral commandments of God? The apostle Paul said that the will of God was our "sanctification" (1 Thessalonians 4:3-7). If we trust God, will we not live the kind of life that distinguishes us from the world? (Matthew 5:13-16, 46-47; 1 Peter 4:3-4).

And how can faith be complete without obedience to the conditions for salvation that are plainly spelled out in the New Testament? There are numerous kinds of faith, but only one faith is powerful and able to save (Ephesians 4:5). The faith that trusts in God is the faith that saves for the simple reason that the power is not within us but within Him. Faith without works relies solely on the believer, but when faith expresses itself in obedience, it reveals a dependence on God who can do all things.

Discussion

1. What are the two sides of the debate over justification by faith?

2. Is there any question about whether salvation comes through faith?

3. What conclusion did Martin Luther draw about the role of faith in justification? What drove him to this conclusion?

4. What is the "Ninety-Five Theses"?

5. What are some of the conditions for salvation according to the New Testament? Can these be reconciled with the doctrine of salvation by faith alone?

6. What does James say about faith alone in James 2:14-26?

7. Do Paul and James contradict one another? How do you explain their perspectives on faith and works?

8. Do demons believe? Why did James bring demons into his discussion of faith and works?

9. What examples does James use for perfected faith?

10. What does trusting Jesus involve for us?

FIVE

THE REASON FOR MIRACLES

"Why, sometimes I've believed as many as six impossible things before breakfast."

-The White Queen in
Through the Looking Glass by Lewis Carroll

Where did the faith of Abraham and Rahab come from? When Abraham raised his knife over his son, how did he know everything would be okay? How did Rahab know that it would be better to side with the Israelites than the king of Jericho? Where did Moses get the courage to stand up to Pharaoh?

At first, Moses was afraid. When he was a young man, he killed an Egyptian and ran for his life to Midian. There, he spent forty years in Midian as a shepherd. As far as he knew, his time as a leader of God's people was over. But God had other plans. One day when he was watching his father-in-law's flocks, a strange sight caught Moses' eye: a bush that was on fire yet not consumed by the flames! He approached it to investigate and heard a voice calling out to him, saying, "Moses, Moses!" God was speaking to him! This burning bush, as it turned out, was the first of many wonderful things Moses would witness. God asked him to deliver His people from bondage in Egypt. Moses protested that the people would not believe that the Lord had really sent him, so God commanded him to throw his staff on the ground. When he did, it became a serpent! Then God told Moses to put his hand inside his cloak. Moses complied, and when he pulled his hand out it was leprous like snow. Moses must have been beside himself, but God instructed him to return his hand to his cloak, and this time when Moses pulled it out his hand was restored. Moses would see the Lord do many other remarkable things. After seeing these supernatural events, how could Moses have doubts?

Abraham, Rahab, and Moses all believed God because they had either directly or indirectly witnessed miracles they could not explain. Miracles are the first of two tools the Lord uses to plant faith in the hearts of men and women. We will get to the second in a few chapters, but first we should discuss the miracles we read about in the Bible.

What Is a Miracle?
It is common for people to call anything amazing a "miracle," such as the birth of the baby or surviving a near-death experience. For the purposes of this lesson, we will stick to the biblical definition of a miracle, which has been well summarized by R.C. Sproule:

> A miracle is an extraordinary work performed by the immediate power of God in the external, perceivable world, which is an act against nature that only God can do, such as bring life out of death or something out of nothing.[1]

Just because something is amazing, that does not make it a miracle. It has to be out of the ordinary, inexplicable by scientific law, to qualify as a biblical miracle.

Four words are used to describe miracles in the New Testament. All four are found in Hebrews 2:3-4:

How shall we escape if we neglect such a great salvation? It was declared at first by the Lord, and it was attested to us by those who heard, while God also bore witness by *signs* and *wonders* and various *miracles* and by *gifts of the Holy Spirit* distributed according to his will. (emphasis mine)

"Miracles" is a common term for us, but it appears only seven times in the New Testament. The word it translates is *dynamis*, from which we get "dynamite." It essentially means "power," but it can also indicate acts of power, such as miracles.[2] Miracles are also called "gifts of the Spirit," or "spiritual gifts" (cf. 1 Corinthians 12:1), since they are "given through the Spirit" (1 Corinthians 12:8). "Wonders" emphasizes the amazement felt by those who witnessed miracles. It is always found in the plural when it is used and joined with our last word, "signs." Appearing more than seventy times in the New Testament, "signs" is the most common term for miracles. Just as ordinary signs communicate important messages, the miracles of the Bible communicate important truths that could not be delivered any other way. Throughout the Bible, God used miracles sparingly, allowing the supernatural to break through the natural only when necessary. At these times, miracles communicated God's Word so that faith could be born in human hearts.

The Reason for Miracles

Identifying the Son of God
What would be your reaction if an unknown person approached you suddenly, saying, "I have a message from God for you!" You would probably try to get away from him

as fast as possible. But what if he said this while inexplicably levitating in the air? You still might feel the urge to run, but your amazement would probably win over your fear long enough for you to hear what the man had to say. His ability to stand on thin air would tell you that there is something special about him.

Jesus performed signs to identify Himself as someone sent by the Father in heaven (John 5:36). If He had come without the signs He performed, no one would have taken His bold claims seriously. He would have remained in their minds the carpenter from Nazareth. But because He worked miracles, those with open hearts knew He was the One they had been waiting for. As Nicodemus said, "Rabbi, we know that you are a teacher come from God, for no one can do these signs that you do unless God is with him" (John 3:2).

To the careful observer, Jesus' miracles simply reflected the truth He tried to communicate to the Pharisees when He said, "My Father is working until now, and I am working.... For whatever the Father does, that the Son does likewise" (John 5:17, 19). In an essay entitled "Miracles," C.S. Lewis explains,

> There is an activity of God displayed throughout creation, a wholesale activity let us say which man refused to recognize. The miracles done by God incarnate, living as a man in Palestine, performed the very same things as this wholesale activity, but at a different speed and on a smaller scale. One of their chief purposes is that men, having seen a thing done by personal power on the small-scale, may recognize, when they see the same thing done on the large-scale, that the power behind it is...the very same person who lived among us 2000 years ago.[3]

Every day God provides wonders according to His natural laws—which is our way of referring to the way He chooses to operate normally in the world. When Jesus taught us to pray, "Give us this day our daily bread" (Matthew 6:11), He was speaking of being grateful for God's non-miraculous providence that puts food on our tables. Miracles are like these daily provisions, "not more wonderful, but less frequent."[4]

When Jesus changed the water into wine at Cana, He was merely speeding up a process that has been going on naturally for centuries. God causes the seed to produce the vine, and with the aid of water, soil, and the sun, the vine turns that water into juice. We may attribute all of this to "science," but we're just hiding God's activity with a technical name. When Christ made water into wine at the wedding, "the mask was off."[5] Christ identified Himself as the Messiah by doing God's activity before the very eyes of the wedding attendants.

Every year farmers sow seed, and God responds by making a little wheat into much wheat. We call it "the laws of nature," but again we are hiding God's activity with naturalistic terminology. When Jesus fed the 5000 with five loaves and two fish, He made a little bread into a lot of bread, just as His Father does every harvest. By doing God's activity close up, among the people, Jesus identified Himself as the Son of God.

Revealing the Word of God
In addition to identifying Jesus as the Son of God, miracles also revealed the Word of God after Jesus ascended into heaven. On the night of His arrest, Jesus promised His apostles that He would send them a Helper, the Spirit of truth, who would guide them into all the truth (John 14:16,

26; 16:13). This promise was only for the apostles. They were the ones who Jesus had chosen to preach the good news by the Holy Spirit (1 Peter 1:12). One of these apostles, Paul, faced critics who claimed he had developed his gospel from another man's teaching. He objected in Galatians, saying, "For I would have you know, brothers, that the gospel that was preached by me is not man's gospel. For I did not receive it from any man, nor was I taught it, but I received it through a revelation of Jesus Christ" (Galatians 1:11-12; cf. 1 Corinthians 2:9-13).

When the apostles and the other inspired writers received the miracle of revelation, they wrote down the words God gave them. This is how we have the Bible. The Bible does not claim to be the work of natural geniuses, like Shakespeare, whom God endowed with the ability to write good books. The Bible claims to be "breathed out by God" (2 Timothy 3:16), a miracle known as "inspiration." If the Bible was simply a book written by really smart writers, it would be no more important than the hundreds of other books written by really smart writers. If it really is the Word of God, it had to be miraculously revealed through the Holy Spirit. We will have more to say about this in the chapter on the inspiration of the Bible.

Confirming the Word of God
The final reason for signs is the confirmation of the Word of God. This is what was meant by Hebrews 2:3-4 when it said that the great salvation was "attested to us by those who heard, while God also bore witness by signs and wonders and various miracles and by gifts of the Holy Spirit distributed according to his will." The miracle of revelation seems to have occurred behind closed doors, out of the sight of the public. We do not know how the inspired writers

looked when they received the word. By all appearances, they may have looked like a normal person who was writing a letter to a friend. Jesus promised the apostles that they would not have to study or worry about remembering what He had taught them because the Spirit would teach them all things and bring to their remembrance all that He had taught them (John 14:26). But that sudden insight or miraculous flash of remembrance probably did not give off any visible sign. That means that the miracle of revelation was not enough. More miracles would have to authenticate God's chosen messengers.

At the end of the book of Mark, we read that after the Lord's ascension, the apostles "went out and preached everywhere, while the Lord worked with them and confirmed the message by accompanying signs" (Mark 16:20). Jesus promised them,

> And these signs will accompany those who believe: in my name they will cast out demons; they will speak in new tongues; they will pick up serpents with their hands; and if they drink any deadly poison, it will not hurt them; they will lay their hands on the sick, and they will recover. (vv. 17-18)

When Philip the evangelist went to Samaria, he encountered a sorcerer named Simon. Simon's dark magic amazed the people in that region until Philip arrived, and they saw the true power of God. Simon's parlor tricks were nothing by comparison. Philip's signs enabled the people to discern between the real messengers and the frauds. Even Simon believed and was baptized (Acts 8:9-13). Spiritual gifts enabled the early Christians to authenticate their message as true and separate it from the noise of competing philosophies and religions that caused so much confusion in the ancient world.

Neither Jesus nor His disciples used their miraculous abilities for reasons other than identification, revelation, or confirmation. When the devil tempted Jesus to command the stones in the wilderness to become bread, Jesus refused, not because He was not hungry. He had been fasting for forty days! If the Lord had acquiesced to the devil's suggestion, He would have abused His miraculous power, cheapening it as a means for filling His belly. God already provides food to His creatures. Jesus did not need to work a miracle to get something to eat. Paul had a coworker named Epaphroditus whom he described as "my brother and fellow worker and fellow soldier" (Philippians 2:25). In his letter to the Philippians, Paul relates how Epaphroditus became so ill he nearly died. It is obvious that Paul was very distressed over the situation. Paul was an apostle with spiritual gifts. Why didn't he heal Epaphroditus? In another letter, Paul writes about how lonely he is in prison because, among other reasons, he had to leave a coworker of his named Trophimus behind because he was sick (2 Timothy 4:20). Paul himself had a "thorn in the flesh" that he asked the Lord to remove, but he was not granted his request (2 Corinthians 12:7). Why didn't Paul heal himself or his valued coworkers? The apostle knew that God had not granted him miraculous power to use for his own benefit. Gifts of healing, tongues, prophecy, and other spiritual gifts served to communicate the Word of God to men and women so that faith might germinate in their hearts and grow.

How Does God Bring Faith Today?
Does God still use miracles to nurture faith in the hearts of believers? The Bible is very clear on this question. Miracles were never intended to be the permanent source of faith. When the Word of God was completed and fully confirmed, miracles ceased.

Paul predicted the end of the miraculous age in 1 Corinthians. In chapter 12, he introduced a problem concerning spiritual gifts in the church at Corinth. Evidently, some gifts were more respected than others (like tongues, for example), and those who possessed only natural gifts, such as helping, teaching, leading, and showing mercy, were feeling inferior to the miracle workers. Paul reminded his readers that they were one body made of many members, and every member was important (v. 27). What he said next probably surprised the tongue speakers and healers at Corinth. He followed his teaching about the importance of every member with a discussion of the temporary nature of miraculous gifts and the permanent nature of natural gifts such as faith, hope, and love. After defining the greatest of these, love, he said:

> Love never ends. As for prophecies, they will pass away; as for tongues, they will cease; as for knowledge, it will pass away. For we know in part and we prophesy in part, but when the perfect comes, the partial will pass away. (1 Corinthians 13:8-10)

Paul is using some terms in unfamiliar ways, so his meaning will take a little explanation.

First of all, notice that he clearly predicted an end to the miraculous age. Prophecies, he said, will "pass away;"

tongues will "cease;" miraculous knowledge will "pass away."

Secondly, two of the miracles that he mentions, "knowledge" and "prophecy," are said to manifest themselves "in part" and are contrasted with "the perfect." In other words, whatever they do, they do not do it completely. They are partial. Miracles like knowledge and prophecy revealed the Word of God, but because they did this in a particular place and at a particular time, they could not reveal it fully to all humanity.

Now, what is meant by "the perfect"? A common interpretation is to look at the perfect as the second coming or heaven, but this does not fit with what is later said about the gifts that "abide" into the perfect age: faith, hope, and love (v. 13). Faith will not be needed in heaven, because faith is "the assurance of things hoped for, the conviction of things not seen" (Hebrews 11:1). As the song goes, when Christ comes back "the faith shall be sight."[6] Faith, which is our conviction in the invisible, will be realized when Christ appears. Likewise, hope will be fulfilled at the second coming and replaced by God's presence. Thus, Paul writes, "Now hope that is seen is not hope. For who hopes for what he sees?" (Romans 8:24). There may be love in heaven, but in the presence of Christ faith and hope as we know it will no longer abide.

What could Paul mean about the "perfect"? In the Bible, "perfect" more often means "complete" than "faultless." Remember that Paul has been contrasting the perfect, whatever it is, with that which is "in part," that is, miracles. That means whatever came through miracles "in part" would come in completed form once the miracles ceased. We have already concluded that miracles revealed the Word of God in part, so that must mean that Paul is talking about the completion of the Word of God. When the Word of God was completed, there was no more need for miracles to reveal and confirm it. Their purpose was finished, so they passed away.[7]

This is consistent with the way miracles were imparted in the first century. The early Christians received the ability to perform miracles in two ways: the baptism of the Holy Spirit and the laying on of the apostles' hands. The baptism of the Holy Spirit occurred only twice, unless we assume Saul of Tarsus also received it (cf. Acts 9:17). The first time, the apostles were "filled" with the Holy Spirit and began to speak in other tongues as the Spirit gave them utterance (Acts 2:1-4). The next recorded instance of Holy Spirit baptism occurs in Acts 10 at the household of Cornelius. While Peter was preaching to Cornelius and his family, "the Holy Spirit fell on all who heard the word" (vv. 44-48). We know that this type of baptism was not commonplace, because when Peter traveled to Jerusalem to report what happened at the household of Cornelius, he described what he had seen as what had happened to him and the apostles "at the beginning" (Acts 11:15). If every Christian was baptized by the Holy Spirit, why did Peter have to go back to the beginning, to Pentecost, for a reference to what he had witnessed at Cornelius's house? Later Paul would write that there is "one baptism" (Ephesians 4:5). Unlike Holy Spirit baptism, baptism in water for the forgiveness of sins is universally required of all believers (Matthew 28:19-20; Acts 2:38).

That leaves us with the laying on of the apostles' hands. In Acts 8, Philip converted a number of Samaritans through the preaching of the gospel, but while Philip himself could work miracles, he evidently could not pass them on to others, for he sent for Peter and John, who were in

Jerusalem, so that they could come down and lay their hands on the people so that they could receive the Holy Spirit. Simon the Sorcerer saw this special ability that only the apostles had and offered Peter and John money so that he could impart miracles too, but Peter sternly rebuked him for his foolishness and commanded him to pray for forgiveness (vv. 14-24). In another example, Paul wrote to the church at Rome, saying that he hoped to have an opportunity to see them soon in person so that he might "impart to you some spiritual gift" (Romans 1:11). Without an apostle like Paul, they would not be able to work miracles. If only apostles had the ability to impart spiritual gifts, when the last Christian who had known an apostle died, miracles died with him.

The end of the miraculous age is no reason to mourn. God had always planned to replace the "partial" spiritual gifts with the "perfect" Word of God (James 1:25). That does not mean we cannot learn anything from the miracles that were performed in the early part of the Christian age. Before we get to the role of God's Word in producing faith, let's look at a few examples of miracles to see how they fostered faith in the hearts of the original disciples.

Discussion

1. What is the first of two tools God uses to plant faith in the hearts of men and women?

2. Give a good biblical definition for miracles.

3. What are the four words used to describe miracles in the New Testament?

4. In what way do Jesus' miracles reflect God's activity in the natural world?

5. Who was the Helper Jesus sent to the apostles to guide them into all the truth?

6. Why did the preaching of the apostles have to be confirmed by signs? What were some of the signs God used to bear witness to their message?

7. Why did Paul heal Epaphroditus or Trophimus when they were sick?

8. Does God use miracles to reveal and confirm His Word today? Explain your answer.

9. How were miracles imparted in the first century?

10. What can we learn from the miracles that were performed in the early part of the Christian age?

SIX

A BELIEVER'S UNBELIEF

"I believe; help my unbelief!"

-Mark 9:24

Some pursuits are relaxed, requiring very little focus. We have all been in the situation where a retail clerk approaches and asks if we need any help. "No, just looking," we say. We may know what we are looking for and just don't want someone hanging over our shoulder while we shop, but we may just want to meander around the store aimlessly to see if something catches our eyes. Collectors know the feeling of going to an antique mall or used bookstore, not really knowing what they are looking for until that special item jumps out and screams "buy me!"

The pursuit of faith is not this kind of pursuit. It must be focused, and sometimes that focus is very difficult to achieve. That was certainly the case of the poor father in Mark 9 who tried to get Jesus' disciples to heal his son who had been possessed by a demon. You can hear the frustration and doubt in his appeal to Jesus on behalf of his family: "But if you can do anything, have compassion on us and help us" (v. 22). Jesus answered his request by casting out the evil spirit that afflicted his only son. His words are interesting: "You mute and deaf spirit, I command you, come out of him and never enter him again" (v. 25). The command was both positive and negative: "come out of him" and "never enter him again." Or you could look at it as a contrast: "come out of him" is what I want you to do, not "enter him again." After presenting such a contrast to the evil spirit, there was no confusion over where Jesus wanted it to go.

Contrasts point us away from one direction and guide us to another. For this reason, they can be very helpful in the challenging pursuit of faith. In fact, Jesus' command to the evil spirit is not the only contrast we find in this story. Three others assisted the father in his pursuit of faith. They will also help anyone else who shares his quest.

Arrogance vs. Helplessness

All three gospel accounts that record this incident place it after the Transfiguration of Jesus, which probably occurred on Mount Hermon (Matthew 17:14-19; Mark 9:14-29; Luke 9:37-42). Jesus had experienced the greatest glory He would receive on earth, only to descend the mountain and find chaos surrounding the nine disciples He had left behind to carry on His business while He was away. The text says that when the crowd saw Jesus they were "greatly amazed." This has led some scholars to believe that Jesus' face was still shining with some of the glory He had experienced on the mountain, just as Moses' face shone with glory when He descended Mount Sinai (cf. Exodus 34:29). But there is no reason to believe Jesus looked any different now than at other points in His life. In fact, He told Peter, James, and John not to tell anybody about what they had seen until after His resurrection (Mark 9:9). It is more likely that the Lord returned sooner than expected and caught His disciples in the act of failure. It was an awkward situation.

What did Jesus find when He came down from the mountain? An argument. The disciples had been trying to cast out a demon with no results, and the scribes, always looking for an opportunity, seized upon their failure to discredit them. When Jesus learned this, He appeared exasperated: "O faithless and twisted generation, how long am I to be with you? How long am I to bear with you?" (Matthew 17:17). Some might be surprised at His reaction. In his controversial essay, "Why I Am Not Christian," Bertrand Russell says that in Christ

> one does find repeatedly a vindictive fury against those people who would not listen to his preaching – an attitude which is not uncommon with preachers, but which does somewhat detract from superlative excellence. You do not, for instance, find that attitude in Socrates. You find him quite bland and urbane towards the people who would not listen to him; and it has come to my mind, far more worthy of the sage to take that line than to take the line of indignation.[1]

Jesus' rebuke is just the kind of "attitude" Russell takes issue with. But is it really a discredit to Jesus that it pains Him to witness the impotence of His disciples? Should Jesus smile when the church fails to carry out His mission? Do we see a flaw in Him as He chastises His disciples, or is this something to admire?

Jesus' disciples were trying to exorcise a demon without prayer.[2] At the end of this account, they turned to Him privately and asked why they were unable to cast out the evil spirit. He told them, "This kind cannot be driven out by anything but prayer" (Mark 9:29). He would not have said this if prayer had been a part of the disciples' attempts to help the father's ailing son. Evidently, they had become so sure of themselves that they tried to cast out the demon with the power of their own words. They may have been invoking the name of Jesus (cf. Mark 9:38; 16:17; Luke

10:17), but they were relying upon themselves. They were self-confident rather than God-confident, and that is why they failed.³

Meanwhile, the father of the demon possessed boy was losing hope. Who could blame him? He had probably been more confident when he first approached Jesus' disciples and made his appeal, but their failure and the argument that ensued with the scribes had discouraged him.

The father explained that his son had a spirit that made him deaf and mute. Whenever it seized him, it threw him down, and he foamed at the mouth and ground his teeth and became rigid. The boy suffered violent convulsions and rolled on the ground. The spirit would often cast them into the fire and into the water to destroy him (Mark 9:17-18, 21-22). Luke says the demon "shattered" the boy (9:39). The NASB understands this to be the effect of the demon leaving the boy's body periodically: "only with difficulty does it leave him, mauling him as it leaves." This was the man's "only child" (Luke 9:38). Many of the symptoms described epilepsy (Matthew 17:15). But this isn't merely epilepsy. Epileptic seizures are not triggered by the appearance of specific individuals (Mark 9:20), and they do not end when rebuked (v. 25). Imagine this poor boy covered with scars, disfigured from convulsions, and maimed by fire. He was just a child, but Satan had thrown his cruel forces against him in a visible demonstration of what he wants to do to all of us.

Jesus asked the man how long the boy had been in this condition. "From childhood," the man replied (Mark 9:21). Jesus, of course, knew how long the boy had suffered, but the question had to be asked to demonstrate to the father and the crowd and the disciples that no one had been able to help this child. He needed them to understand how much the father was asking. In other words, the father needed to come to grips with his own hopelessness before Jesus helped him. God always cultivates a dependence, a longing for help, an understood need for a Savior within the hearts of those He delivers before He heals them so that faith might be the means through which He saves. Why do you think we have the Old Testament? Doesn't the first thirty-nine books of the Bible teach us that we cannot possibly help ourselves? When we read about the failures of the patriarchs and the Israelites, are we not reading about our own failures, and isn't the declaration, "None is righteous, no, not one" (Romans 3:10), proven in the centuries from Eden to Christ? This helplessness is necessary. Without it, we would not know where to look in our pursuit of faith.

Doubt vs. Faith
Now in a state of helplessness, knowing that Jesus is the only hope for his son, the father says, "If you can do anything, have compassion on us and help us" (Mark 9:22). Jesus throws the man's words back in his face in an astonishing rebuke: "'If you can!' All things are possible for the one who believes" (v. 23).

What did Jesus mean by "all things?" That the father, or anyone else for that matter, can accomplish anything they desire as long as they trust in Jesus to make it happen? First of all, we should point out that Jesus' promise to the father is not the same as the mountain-moving He promised His disciples later in Matthew 17:20. This man was not an apostle; he had not been commissioned by the Lord to heal the sick and perform miracles. He was an average person, like you and me, so the words Jesus spoke to him apply to all people. However, it is a mistake to take Jesus' promise in the sense that we can have anything we want as long as we have faith. What if the man trusted Jesus to heal his son and send the demon into one of the scribes to get revenge against their heartlessness? Would Jesus have done that? Of course not! That would have been inconsistent with His character and purposes. Besides, what about all of the sick and afflicted who make legitimate appeals to God in prayer through faith and never receive the healing they asked for? Do we challenge their belief? Do we conclude that God does not exist? There has to be another explanation.

Jesus did not tell the man that all things would be done for the one who believes, but that all things are "possible." And that truth has more to do with the believer than with Jesus. Jesus was not defending God's ability to do great things; He was trying to correct a deficit in the man's faith. He wanted the man to start believing in possibilities again. Commenting on this verse, William Barclay wrote, "To approach anything in the spirit of hopelessness is to make it hopeless; to approach anything in the spirit of faith is to make it a possibility."[4] Faith makes all things possible. Faith is not knowing what God *will do* but knowing He *can do* anything. That doesn't mean that if you believe you will get anything that you ask from God. It does mean that those who believe have hope and will not give in to despair.

The possibility for the boy's healing depended upon his father's faith. Why? Was Jesus unable to heal unbelievers? Certainly not. The blind man in John 9 did not even know that it was Jesus who had healed him. The widow at Nain did not seem to have faith before Jesus raised her son from the dead, and her son, of course, could not have believed (Luke 7:11-17). Modern-day faith healers will blame their failures on subjects who don't have faith, appealing to passages such as this, but the condition of faith was not meant to empower Jesus. Actually, it accomplished two things. It kept Jesus from wasting His efforts on unbelievers who would never repent, and it also served in this case as an incentive to the father to get rid of the doubt implied in his weak appeal.[5]

The father immediately cried out in his anguish and helplessness: "I believe!" And then, with a sudden awareness of how hollow those words were, he added, "Help my unbelief!" (Mark 9:24). Did the man believe or didn't he? Contrary to the way the man's words look on the surface, he was actually rounding the corner in his pursuit of faith. There is doubt here, but it is different from the doubt implied in his first appeal to Jesus. His words now are marked with real belief. His faith is weak, but it is directed at the right person. And now that he has it, he realizes how faltering his faith really is. It is not until you have faith that you are able to measure your doubts. Only true believers understand the depths of their own doubts. It is natural for us to struggle, especially during difficult trials. The dangerous doubt was not in the man's cry for help but in his earlier appeal to Christ that hinged on the word "if."

If you can bring yourself to cry out to God with the word "help" and leave out the word "if," that is enough. Jesus would heal this man's son, not because his father was perfect, but because his father sensed his helplessness and was penitent in the face of his own doubt.

Mountains vs. Mustard Seeds

If Jesus had been set apart from His disciples on the Mount of Transfiguration where He shone with a heavenly brilliance and conversed with Elijah and Moses while a voice from heaven boomed a command to listen to Him, He really stood out from them as He approached the boy who was still as a corpse, took his hand, and led him to his father. Jesus could bathe in glory on the mountain and come down into the valley of suffering with the same passion and focus. On the other hand, Peter seemed to want to stay on the mountaintop, away from the suffering and doubts of humanity. Too many of us are like Peter and want to build our shrines away from the world's sin and pain, but before we can rescue the lost, we must go to where they are.[6]

After Jesus cast the demon out of the young boy, His disciples took Him aside privately to ask Him why they were not able to cast it out. "This kind cannot be driven out by anything but prayer," He said (Mark 9:29). Evidently the disciples had attempted to perform a supernatural act without praying to God! It is no wonder that they failed. Prayer was necessary, not because it imparted power, but because it intensified their faith which enabled them to fully exert the power Christ had already imparted to them.[7]

In Matthew's account, Jesus explains, telling them they have "little faith." He says, "For truly, I say to you, if you have faith like a grain of mustard seed, you will say to this mountain, 'Move from here to there,' and it will move, and nothing will be impossible for you" (Matthew 17:20). As I said earlier, this advice differs from Jesus' encouragement to the father. He is speaking to His apostles, who had been given miraculous abilities. But these abilities depended on prayer-intensified faith.

Jesus used the metaphor of a mustard seed a number of times in his ministry. Sometimes He used it to describe living faith, alluding to the potential and vitality of a mustard seed (cf. Luke 17:6; 1 Corinthians 13:2). But here He plays on the smallness of the mustard seed, which is a very small thing when compared with a mountain.[8] Even little faith in the right object is enough to move mountains.

I don't believe that Jesus was talking about literal mountains, and I wouldn't expect you to be naïve enough to make that conclusion, either. Why would His disciples want to level mountains? They weren't in the construction business. The mountains are figurative, standing for the seemingly insurmountable barriers we often face, barriers, like a child who is impossibly sick, whom no doctors can seem to help. All of us face barriers in our lives that challenge us. Sometimes we allow these barriers to stop cold our pursuit of faith. Jesus is telling us to allow for possibilities. All things are possible with God. Don't look at life as a pessimist who doesn't believe. You may have doubts but believe just enough to know that hope is possible. Little as it is, that faith will be your salvation.

Discussion

1. Can the pursuit of faith to be aimless?

2. What special event preceded the miracle in this chapter?

3. What failure did Jesus have to address when He came down from the mountain?

4. Did Jesus get frustrated with His disciples? Is this a flaw or something to admire?

5. Why is it important for us to understand that we cannot possibly help ourselves?

6. What did Jesus mean when He told the father that all things are possible for the one who believes?

7. Was Jesus unable to heal people who did not believe in Him?

8. Can true believers have doubts? What role does doubt play in the pursuit of faith?

9. Why must we come down from our "mountaintops" to places where people are hurting and struggling?

10. Why did the disciples need prayer to cast out the demon?

SEVEN

LONG DISTANCE HEALING

"Faith may be true, and yet most capable of...increase."
-R.C. Trench

Faith comes in different shapes and sizes. It always starts small. Jesus talked about faith "like a grain of mustard seed," a small seed with potential to become a tree large enough for the birds of the air to nest in its branches (Matthew 17:20). Faith can stagnate and grow cold or grow to be dynamic and vibrant. It can grow in the wrong direction. John Reynell Wreford's hymn expresses the remedy for diminishing faith:

> When my love for Christ grows weak,
> When for deeper faith I seek,
> Then in thought I go to thee,
> Garden of Gethsemane.[1]

If faith can go in the wrong direction, it can also grow in the right direction. R.C. Trench said, "Faith may be true, and yet most capable of...increase."[2] The Bible is full of examples of believers who continued to grow in faith. After the first miracle when Jesus turned water into wine, Jesus' disciples believed on Him (John 2:11), yet, being "disciples," they must have already enjoyed some level of belief. In Luke 17:5 it was the apostles who prayed, "Increase our faith!" The Israelites who followed Moses through the Red Sea already believed in God and had seen His power, but after Pharaoh was overthrown we read that they "believed in the Lord and in his servant Moses" (Exodus 14:31). The faithful widow whose son Elijah raised from the dead cried, "Now I know that you are a man of God, and that the word of the Lord in your mouth is truth" (1 Kings 17:24).

Whether your faith is absent, stagnant, growing in the wrong direction, or strong, there is hope for even stronger faith. Such was the case in the life of an official whose son became critically ill and who sought the Lord Jesus for help. He was an important man from Caesarea, the Roman capital of Palestine. We do not know what kind of "official" he was. Perhaps he was an officer in the administration of Herod Antipas, who was tetrarch of Galilee. His story is an example of how the Lord used miracles not only to plant faith in human hearts, but also to strengthen it.

Faith doesn't come all at once in a neat little package. It grows in stages. It may be helpful to trace these stages through the official's experience with Jesus.

Stage One

The official was running out of options. His son was at the point of death, and evidently nobody else could help him. When he heard Jesus had come from Judea to Galilee, he "went to him and asked him to come down and heal his son..." (v. 47). J.W. McGarvey believes that the literal phrasing contains a "delicate suggestion that the father was reluctant to leave the son, even to seek aid."[3]

In a sense, the son did his father a favor. The father would not have been curious about Jesus if his son had not fallen ill. I have heard Christians express doubts about their faith because of the fortuitous circumstances surrounding their introduction to Christianity. Maybe they had been born in a Christian home. Maybe a near death experience woke them up. Maybe they first started coming to church because they were interested in a guy or a girl. In other words, they had doubts because their first contact with Jesus did not come about for strictly spiritual reasons. Earlier in John 4, the Samaritans "believed because of his word" (v. 41). They were not responding to a crisis or a miracle when they encountered Jesus, and His teaching was enough. It was different with the official. Tragedy brought him to the Lord. Who is to say one way of coming to Jesus is better than another? With Paul we should say, "By the grace of God I am what I am" (1 Corinthians 15:10) regardless of the circumstances surrounding our introduction to Christ.

The nouns in verse 46 are interesting. We have an "official," but his position and riches could not save him from tragedy. He has a "son" (*paidion*), but although he was young it seemed his father would outlive him. They are in "Capernaum," the city of consolation, yet they were in great sorrow. Neither position, nor youth, nor location could save them. Jesus was all they had left.[4]

The official had faith, but it was feeble because it limited Christ in two ways.

It limited Christ's power to His presence.
Jesus was in Cana; the official was from Capernaum. He asked Jesus to "come down and heal his son." It had not occurred to him that Jesus could have healed the boy remotely.

Contrast the official from Capernaum with another official, the Roman centurion in Matthew 8. The centurion is often confused with the official in our text, but there are major differences. The centurion had a servant who was sick, but the official in our story had a son. Furthermore, when the centurion appealed to Jesus, he did not ask Jesus to come to his home. Instead he said,

> Lord, I am not worthy to have you come under my roof, but only say the word, and my servant will be healed. For I too am a man under authority, with soldiers under me. And I say to one, go, and he goes, and to another, come, and he comes, and to my servant, do this, and he does it. (Matthew 8:8-9)

When Jesus heard this, "he marveled and said to those who followed him, truly, I tell you, with no one in Israel have I found such faith" (v. 10).

It limited Christ's power to the living.
In haste, the official pled with Jesus, "Sir, come down before my child dies" (v. 49). It never occurred to him that Jesus could have helped even if the young boy had died. Of course, we are being judgmental. Would we have believed any differently?

The Lord began to strengthen the official's faith right away with a rebuke: "Unless you see signs and wonders you will not believe" (v. 48). Jesus was disappointed that people were so reluctant to believe without miracles. Miracles were necessary in the beginning to establish Jesus' identity and confirm His message, but they were never meant to be a continuous spring feeding faith as they are considered by some today. Today God creates faith using His Word. We will have more to say on that in chapters 10-12.

Unlike the Samaritans in Sychar, the official would not believe until he could "see" Jesus' miraculous power. The official, not Jesus, was the one suffering from limitations. His faith was limited to the external, outward, and physical.

He was not unlike the multitude Jesus fed with five loaves and two fish to whom He said:

> Truly, truly, I say to you, you are seeking me, not because you saw signs, but because you ate your fill of the loaves. Do not labor for the food that perishes, but for the food that endures to eternal life, which the Son of Man will give to you. For on him God the Father has set his seal. (John 6:26-27)

He was not unlike Thomas who demanded to place his finger into the mark of the nails in Jesus' hand and into the scar on Jesus' side before he would believe in Jesus' resurrection. After Jesus gave him that opportunity, the Lord said, "Have you believed because you have seen me? Blessed are those who have not seen and yet have believed" (John 20:29).

Stage Two

Jesus used two terms in the text for what He was about to do for the official (v. 48). The first, "signs," indicated that miracles were never about themselves but pointed to something deeper. It took a level of faith not yet attained by the official to see miracles as signs. Nicodemus had this faith because he said, "No one can do these signs that you do unless God is with him" (John 3:2). The second, "wonders," probably reflected the level of faith possessed by the official at this time. The word indicates the astonishment miracles caused by their strangeness.

To the official's credit, when Jesus told him, "Go; your son will live," the man "believed [for the first time] the word that Jesus spoke to him and went on his way," even though at first he wanted Jesus to come to his house (v. 50). This shows a maturation in the official's faith.

Isaiah 28:16 says, "Whoever believes will not be in haste." If there was any sign of desperation or hurry in the official, John did not record it. The official seems to have found peace in the second stage of his faith. He now believed Jesus was able to heal his son even though He was ten miles away.

This may have been the point of conversion for the official. It was a "start" (see NASB). Isn't that what conversion is? A start? You are not supposed to be fully grown at conversion. Obeying the gospel results in a "new birth" (John 3:3, 5). We start out as babes in Christ.

How much do I need to know in order to obey the gospel? Some people who have been Christians for years begin to have doubts about their conversion because of how much they have grown over time. They see a big difference between who they are now and who they were at the time of their conversion. That is the way it should be. How much did the multitude on Pentecost know after hearing one gospel sermon? (Acts 2). How much did the Philippian jailer know? (Acts 16:25-34). What about the Ethiopian eunuch? (Acts 8:26-40). If you know the danger of sin, the necessity of the blood of Jesus Christ, God's plan of salvation, and the faithfulness expected of you after conversion, you know enough to become a child of God.

However, we are supposed to grow. There is something physically wrong with a person who remains a baby. The same is true spiritually. If we are not growing, our faith will not be strong enough to prevail (1 Corinthians 3:1-3; Hebrews 5:12-14; 2 Peter 3:18).

Stage Three

Jesus orchestrated the events so that the official's faith would grow at an optimal rate. As we have said, Jesus did not go with the official to his house but healed him long distance. As the man returned home, his servants met him with news that his son was recovering. So the official asked them the hour when his son "began to get better" (John 4:52). This is an important point. His question suggests he was looking for a slow recovery, something closer to the natural way of healing. But the servants' answer indicated an immediate recovery: "Yesterday at the seventh hour the fever left him" (v. 52). It was the same time Jesus told him that his son would live!

The man's inquiry was an important factor in his spiritual growth. Most of us would have been satisfied with the news that the son was recovering. The servants would not have thought to give the exact time of the recovery. But the official began to take the controls of his spiritual growth away from Christ and into his own hands and questioned further. As a result, he learned that Jesus was able to heal his son immediately from a long distance.

This example is a divine commendation on the role of Apologetics in Christian faith. We have nothing to fear from asking big questions like: "Where did we come from?" "Does the Bible bear the marks of inspiration?" "Is there evidence that Jesus rose from the dead?" "Are there arguments favoring the existence of God?" As we grow, we must push further, ready to give an answer to anyone who asks for a reason for the hope that is in us (1 Peter 3:15).

The official saved no one but himself with Stage 2 faith, but he saved his whole household when he reached Stage 3! (John 4:53). Our faith must grow, if not for any other reason, to give others the same hope of salvation our faith brings to us. We must reach our children, neighbors, coworkers, classmates, family, friends, and anyone who will listen! This is our mission! (Mark 16:15). Strong faith is required for us to fulfill it.

Faith rarely grows smoothly and gradually. Spiritual growth often faces setbacks. It lurches forward and then comes to a grinding halt. It progresses in fits and starts. But if you have been growing spiritually, you should be able to tell. Look back over the last year or so. See yourself in the past. Are you the same person? Stagnant faith will have left you in the same place. But if your faith has grown, you will see a difference.

A different official than the one who left his ailing son came home to Capernaum from Jesus. Jesus had strengthened his faith in a remarkable way. He left as a man who needed to see signs and wonders, but he returned as a man who had the kind of faith that leads others to Christ without the need for visible demonstrations.

Discussion

1. Give some examples of different kinds of faith.

2. Will your faith ever mature to the point that it no longer needs to grow?

3. Is one way of coming to Jesus any better than another?

4. In what two ways did the official's weak faith limit Christ?

5. How is the official different from the centurion in Matthew 8?

6. What two terms did Jesus use to describe the miracle He performed on the official's son? What is the significance of these terms?

7. How much does a person need to know to obey the gospel?

8. What is Apologetics? What role should it play in the development of Christian faith?

9. How can growing faith aid our evangelistic efforts?

10. Look back over the last year or so. Is your faith growing? What can you do now to ensure that it will continue to grow in the future?

EIGHT

WALKING TREES

"He has sent me to proclaim liberty to the captives and recovering of sight to the blind...."

-Luke 4:18

Mark is the only gospel writer who records a strange encounter with Jesus in Bethsaida:

> And they came to Bethsaida. And some people brought to him a blind man and begged him to touch him. And he took the blind man by the hand and led him out of the village, and when he had spit on his eyes and laid his hands on him, he asked him, "Do you see anything?" And he looked up and said, "I see people, but they look like trees, walking." Then Jesus laid his hands on his eyes again; and he opened his eyes, his sight was restored, and he saw everything clearly. And he sent him to his home, saying, "Do not even enter the village." (Mark 8:22-26)

Perhaps the other gospel writers declined to use this miracle out of the hundreds, maybe thousands, available to them because the blind man whom Jesus healed did not receive his sight all at once.[1] Perhaps Matthew, Luke, and John did not want their readers to misunderstand. This miracle has nothing to do with any weakness on Jesus' part. Like with every other miracle He performed, He was in full control of the healing down to the last detail. The blind man in Bethsaida recovered just the way Jesus wanted him to.

The man's gradual recovery may have been important to the structure of Mark's account. Mark has been talking about the disciples' lack of understanding (8:21). With the account of the man who recovers his eyesight in Bethsaida, Mark begins a major section in his gospel that deals with the disciples' comprehension of Jesus Christ (8:22-10:52). Peter is a good representation for what was going on in the rest of the disciples' hearts. After the blind man was healed, Peter confessed that Jesus was the Christ (8:29). But he was only beginning to fully understand who Jesus was. Soon afterwards, Peter stood in Jesus' way (vv. 32-33). It is no coincidence that this section of Mark ends with another healing of a blind man. Mark wants his readers to identify with Peter and the other disciples who were struggling to see who Jesus really was and grow in their faith.[2]

Regardless of why Mark chose to include this particular miracle, the story surrounding it is a touching tale of friends once again bringing someone they love to Jesus because of an affliction (cf. 7:32). We do not have too many clues concerning the blind man's faith, but his friends clearly believed Jesus was the answer to every problem, no matter how insurmountable it seemed.

When the friends brought the blind man to Jesus, they may have been surprised by how strange this miracle was. They must have been happy with the results, but they could never have guessed how Jesus would bring light to the eyes of this man who had been in darkness. Four strange details stand out.

The Spit

Mark says, "When he had spit on his eyes and laid his hands on him, he asked him, 'Do you see anything?'" (v. 23). This is not the first time Jesus used saliva to heal someone (Mark 7:33; John 9:6). In this case, most of us imagine Jesus spitting on His hands, rubbing them together, and applying the moisture to the poor man's eyes. That image is enough to make most of us wince, but Mark's language suggests that Jesus spit on his closed eyelids while holding him still with His hands![3]

It may be hard to believe, but spit was a common remedy in those times. Pliny the Elder, who was a contemporary of Jesus, reported that saliva was used, among other things, as an antidote for snake venom, a preventative measure against epilepsy, an application for boils, a topical solution to treat leprosy, a way of strengthening the hands, a treatment for a crick in the neck, medicine for various cancers, and, yes, a salve for eye diseases.[4]

Jesus may have been following the medical practices of the time to make His observers more comfortable with placing the blind man into His care. Just as King Hezekiah was told to apply a poultice of the figs to his wound (Isaiah 33:21) and the disciples were told to anoint the sick with oil in the limited commission (Mark 6:13), the Lord used the medicine of the time to clothe His supernatural healing. Some of these techniques may have been helpful; some of them, as here, were obviously ineffectual. Today, God still uses modern medicine to heal, and we are grateful for it, but we must remember that ultimately God is always the healer. He can heal directly, or He can heal through other means.

It is important for us to pray for the sick no matter how good the care. We may live in an age of modern medicine and sophisticated technology, but that does not change the fact that all healing comes from on high.

Another reason Jesus spit on the blind man may have had something to do with a well-attested Jewish superstition that saliva protected against magic and demons.[5] Jesus did not believe in these silly notions. He may have spit into the eyes He was about to restore as a way of proving that His power did not come from the demonic world or black magic. His power was behind everything that is good in the world, and it was greater than any other force.

Perhaps this physical contact with the man whom Jesus was meant to show Jesus' personal interest in people regardless of their station in life. Mark says the friends who brought the blind man to Jesus "begged him to touch him" (v. 22). Physical contact shows compassion. On another occasion, Jesus even touched a leper! (Mark 1:41). Leprosy was believed to be an extremely contagious disease, and contact with someone afflicted with leprosy rendered a person unclean (Leviticus 13:45-46). Physical contact, even with a leper, was worth the risk for Jesus because He wanted to show compassion. He does not heal us from afar. He knows how many hairs are on each of our heads and takes a personal interest in all our plights.

The Walking Trees

The most fascinating part of the story is the man's comment that upon first seeing, he saw people, but they looked to him like trees, walking. Obviously, the Lord was not done healing him. Perhaps men, women, and animals were walking along the road with huge loads of brushwood, thorn bushes, and branches, so large that he could not see who was carrying them. Maybe he was so nearsighted that heads appeared to him like treetops.

Why didn't the man see clearly immediately? Was his faith the problem? Modern day faith healers excuse failed attempts to heal the sick, arguing that those who were not healed did not have enough faith (cf. Mark 6:5-6). In the New Testament, there are several cases in which people without faith received healing, the most amazing of which involved the dead! (Mark 5:41-42; Luke 7:14-15; John 11:43-44). There has never been a case in which Jesus could not help someone who came to Him to be healed. The only people Jesus could not help were the people who did not want His help.

If the blind man was not the problem, was it Jesus' fault that the man was seeing walking trees instead of people? Not necessarily. Perhaps the walking trees were not a mistake but a part of Jesus' plan. The next strange detail explains.

The Gradual Healing

The healing came in stages: On the first attempt, the man saw walking trees where he should have seen people. Then Jesus laid His hands on his eyes again, and this time "the man's sight was restored, and he saw everything clearly" (v. 25). Why didn't Jesus heal the man all at once?

When reading stories in the Bible like this one, we must be careful not to read too much into them. But we also must be careful not to read too little. There is a reason why the Holy Spirit included this little tale in Mark's gospel.

First of all, it is possible that Jesus desired to create a longing in the man so that He could impress him more deeply with the power of God.[6] As we have already noticed, Jesus' miracles did not depend on the man's faith. It was the other way around: the man's faith depended on His miracles. Jesus was not just healing a man or impressing a crowd. He worked miracles to enable and strengthen faith.

Furthermore, doesn't the blind man's experience reflect the way we gradually come into a relationship with God? It doesn't happen all at once. At first we do not see clearly; much of the old blindness remains. But as we continue in faithfulness, we learn more and see more. Just as in the story of the blind man, Jesus thankfully doesn't stop with the first distribution of grace, but in James' words, "he gives more grace" (James 4:6). He is the "author and finisher of our faith" (Hebrews 12:2, KJV).[7]

Finally, if our theory about the organization of Mark is correct, Jesus' miracle served as a parable of what He was doing for the disciples who struggled to understand who He truly was (cf. v. 21). Just as physical light gradually dawned in the man's eyes, spiritual illumination was gradually dawning in the hearts of the apostles.

Jesus was in full control. On many other occasions He had proven His ability to heal completely in the blink of an eye. Now He did something unique to reflect the nature of true faith in the heart of the believer. We should not expect to be born again with a full-grown faith. Faith comes gradually, over a lifetime. It comes in stages.

The Instruction Not to Enter the Village

Before He healed the blind man, Jesus took him by the hand and led him out of the village (v. 23). After the man recovered his sight, Jesus sent him home with a prohibition: "Do not even enter the village" (v. 26). Jesus gave similar orders on other occasions (Matthew 9:30; Mark 1:44; 7:36). It is hard to say exactly why He did not want the man to go into the village and report his good news. Perhaps he wanted the result of the miracle to speak for itself. Boasting pales in comparison to the works of God.

Whatever the reason, we must understand that Jesus' instructions were limited to particular circumstances in the case of a particular blind man. He has given us no such instructions. On the contrary, we are to tell as many people as possible about our healing. As Christians saved through the blood of Christ, we are "under obligation" to tell the world how it also can be saved (Romans 1:14). Jesus left us with the Great Commission to go into all the world and make disciples of all nations (Matthew 28:19-20). We are to enter the village, the neighborhood, the workplace, the school, the home, the city, and any other place where lost souls may listen to God's good news.

This is a story of gradual healing. The Lord is not done with any of us yet. No one has sinned to the point that he or she cannot be healed again. No one has reached full growth. No one is fully mature in Christ. We are growing together, like the man Jesus healed in Bethsaida.

Discussion

1. Did the gradual healing of the blind man indicate weakness on Jesus' part? Why do you think Jesus healed the man in stages?

2. Why do you think Jesus spit on the blind man's eyes?

3. Why do you think the blind man first saw trees, walking?

4. Should we continue to pray for the sick even though we live in the age of modern medicine?

5. Give some reasons why Jesus chose not to heal the blind man all at once.

6. How did Jesus' miracles enable and strengthen faith?

7. Does faith come upon us all at once? Or does it grow gradually, as the blind man's eyesight was restored gradually?

8. How could the blind man's experience be looked at as a parable of the disciples' growing faith?

9. What instructions did Jesus give the blind man after he was healed? Why do you think Jesus gave him this command?

10. How do Jesus' instructions to us compare with the ones given to the blind man? Do we have different orders?

NINE

THE MAN WHO HAD DIED

"Every parting gives a foretaste of death; every coming together again a foretaste of the resurrection."
-Arthur Schopenhauer

It is easier to build something from scratch than to remodel. Anybody who has ever tried to hang a new door, patch a ceiling, or even paint a wall knows that this is true. Whenever a contractor builds a new house, he starts with the bare ground and is able to build what he wants, according to his own blueprints, with few impediments to stand in his way. When a homeowner remodels, he has to work around years of previous construction. He may not be able to construct exactly what he originally planned. When someone has been there first, you have to adapt.

The same situation occurs in evangelism. If the church had been dropped into a world where everyone was a blank slate looking for the truth, we would have no problem teaching the lost. But that kind of world is a fantasy. As the church, the Great Commission sends us into a world full of people with preconceived notions, inherited traditions, and competing religious faiths that have to be torn down before the gospel can be delivered.

Thankfully, Jesus modeled how to reach the lost in this environment. When He came to earth, He had to break down all kinds of prejudices and preconceived notions in order to show the world who He truly was, even with His friends.

Bethany was a little village that was often frequented by Jesus and His disciples on their journeys to Jerusalem. It was near to the city, so it was a convenient stop for them. What made it more inviting was the presence of Lazarus and his two sisters, Mary and Martha, who were dear friends of Jesus.

So when Jesus received a message from the sisters saying that their brother was ill, His disciples probably assumed that He would leave for Bethany immediately, despite the fact that the Jews were seeking to stone Him. However, instead of leaving immediately, Jesus stayed two days longer where He was until He knew that Lazarus was dead. Jesus' delay was not motivated by cruelty. In fact, John notes that "Jesus loved Martha and her sister and Lazarus," and his language suggests that His love was the very reason why Jesus waited as long as He did: "*So* when he heard that Lazarus was ill, he stayed two days longer in the place where he was" (vv. 5-6, emphasis added). Jesus hesitated because of His love for this family!

The Lord had to correct some misunderstandings regarding His glory, and the shock of death was the only thing powerful enough to awaken His friends to reality. He said to His disciples, "This illness does not lead to death. It is for the glory of God, so that the Son of God may be glorified through it" (v. 4). After He was sure that Lazarus was dead, He said to the disciples, "And for your sake I am glad that I was not there, so that you may believe" (v. 15). The disciples may have responded that they already believed and that they did not understand how letting Lazarus die would help their faith. They did believe to a degree, but they had not come to the realization of the full glory of Jesus, nor would they until they visited Lazarus's tomb.

Jesus had a lot of work to do. He was dealing with more than one kind of misinformed faith. John concentrates on the misunderstandings of the two sisters. Both came to Jesus, saying, "Lord, if you had been here, my brother would not have died" (vv. 21, 32), but behind their tearful statements were two different ideas about who Jesus was. Neither was correct.

Martha's Faith

By the time Jesus arrived in Bethany, Lazarus had already been dead four days (v. 17). Martha came out to meet Him first, saying, "Lord, if you had been here, my brother would not have died. But even now I know that whatever you ask from God, God will give you" (vv. 21-22). At first glance, it seems that she really believed Jesus could bring her brother back from the dead, but there are a few clues that point to shortcomings in her faith. First of all, her wording in verse 22 betrays that while she believed Jesus to be a prophet, she did not think that He was God. The word translated "ask" is *aiteisthai*, a word that is always used of the inferior asking something of a superior. Jesus often spoke of asking the Father for things, but He never used this word. He always used *eroto*, which denotes an equality between the asker and the one being asked (John 14:16; 16:26; 17:9, 15, 20).[1] To Martha, Jesus may have been someone special, a prophet maybe, but He still wasn't equal to God.

Also, consider Martha's behavior when they came to her brother's tomb. When Jesus asked the men to take away the stone from the opening of the tomb, Martha protested, "Lord, by this time there will be an odor, for he has been dead four days" (v. 39). Why would she make this comment if she really believed Jesus was about to raise her brother from the dead?

Jesus reassured her, "Your brother will rise again," but Martha fell back on the assurances she no doubt had been receiving from her Jewish friends over the last few days: "I know that he will rise again in the resurrection on the last day" (v. 24). That was when Jesus said, "I am the resurrection and the life. Whoever believes in me, though he die, yet shall he live" (v. 25). This is one of the seven "I am" statements in the book of John. It is important for two reasons. First of all, in using the phrase "I am," Jesus was making a bold claim of divinity. "I am" is the name that God gave to Moses at the burning bush when Moses asked His name (Exodus 3:14). It is the phrase that caused the Pharisees to hurl stones at Jesus, trying to kill Him (John 8:58). It was dangerous to use this phrase in this manner because a person would only do that if he thought he was God. The second reason why Jesus' statement was important is that while Martha believed that He had special power as an inferior who could ask God for life, Jesus claimed to be life itself.[2] He wasn't just going to ask God to give Lazarus life; He Himself would grant her brother his life.

Jesus asked Martha, "Do you believe this?" In response, she made the Good Confession: "Yes, Lord; I believe that you are the Christ, the Son of God, who is coming into the world" (v. 27; cf. Matthew 16:16; John 6:14). The verb is in the perfect tense: "I have believed and still believe." Martha did not see any difference between what she thought and what Jesus was teaching her. She remained steadfast in her position. She would stay there unless something remarkable shook the very foundations of her world.

Mary's Faith

We have come to expect more out of Mary than her sister. Luke's portrait of the two sisters has Martha as the distracted, rule-oriented sister who was more worried about getting food on the table than hearing Jesus' teaching. Meanwhile Mary sat at Jesus' feet, choosing "the good portion, which will not be taken away from her" (Luke 10:38-42). As John begins to tell the story about Lazarus, he reminds us that this was the Mary "who anointed the Lord with ointment and wiped his feet with her hair" (John 11:2; cf. 12:3).

But it was Martha, not Mary, who first went out to meet Jesus. It was only at her sister's prompting that Mary rose from where she had been weeping and went out to Jesus, repeating her sister's line: "Lord, if you had been here, my brother would not have died" (v. 32).

Mary's weeping was heavy with sorrow. John said that when Jesus saw her tears and those of the others "he was deeply moved in his spirit" (v. 33). The phrase originally meant "to snort with anger like a horse."[3] It is used three other times in the New Testament (Matthew 9:30; Mark 1:43; 14:5), and in each case it represents a scolding, a stern warning, or something said in indignation.[4] Jesus seemed to be sincerely agitated over the pain that sin had brought into the world (cf. Romans 5:12; 1 Corinthians 15:26). Not only was the Lord "deeply moved," but He was also "greatly troubled." It is possible that John means to say Jesus visibly shook as He fought to control His emotions.[5] Next, in a two-word statement, John expresses Jesus' human side better than any lengthy sermon or verbose book could: "Jesus wept" (v. 35). The verb indicates silent tears.

Why did Jesus cry? He could not have been distraught over Lazarus' death. Several of the statements He made prior to His visit to the tomb indicate that He knew Lazarus would live again (cf. vv. 4, 11, 25). Furthermore, Jesus knew that, physically dead, Lazarus was in a better place (Psalm 116:15; Philippians 1:21-23). Jesus wept because of His sympathy for Mary, Martha, and the others. John clearly stated that the Lord's emotions were stirred "when Jesus saw her weeping, and the Jews who had come with her also weeping" (v. 33). The Son of God came to earth and cried with mortal men and women! He sympathizes with us! (Hebrews 4:15). Our Lord was compassionate at the tomb of Lazarus, and He sees *our* tears as well. The psalmist pictures God bottling up our tears and recording our sorrows in a book (Psalm 56:8). We serve a God who cares!

Unlike Martha, Mary did not want to talk about resurrection. There is very little conversation between her and Jesus at all, except for a repetition of her sister's statement that if Jesus had been there, their brother would not have died. We may have some clue as to the state of her heart in verse 37, where some of her friends remark, "Could not he who opened the eyes of the blind man also have kept this man from dying?" Perhaps Mary was upset because while her sister entertained doubts about Jesus' power, she had concerns over His compassion. Why did she and her sister and her brother's loved ones have to hurt so much? She was about to find out.

Jesus' Reality
Ignoring Martha's protests, Jesus had the stone moved from the opening of Lazarus' tomb and said, "Did I not tell you that if you believed you would see the glory of God?" He prayed so that the witnesses could hear: "Father, I thank you that you have heard me. I knew that you always hear me, but I said this on account of the people standing around,

that they may believe that you sent me" (vv. 41-42). Then Jesus cried out with a loud voice, "Lazarus, come out." John, no doubt, was at a loss for words: "The man who had died came out, his hands and feet bound with linen strips, and his face wrapped with a cloth." There was no need for Jesus to say anything; the miraculous sign said it all. After ordering the man to unbind him and let him go, Jesus went on His way (vv. 43-44).

John may not have been able to capture the emotions he felt on that occasion, but he was very specific about who came out of that tomb: "the man who had died." This was not a ghost. In Dickinson's *A Christmas Carol*, Ebenezer Scrooge's former partner, Jacob Marley, comes back from the dead. When Scrooge asks, "Who are you?" The ghost replies, "Ask me who I was." "Who were you then?" said Scrooge. "In life I was your partner, Jacob Marley."[6] Ghosts are not real, but even if they were, they would not be anything like Lazarus. The phantom Scrooge encountered had once been Jacob Marley. The man who came out of the tomb was fully Lazarus! The same man who befriended Jesus and loved his sisters came out of the tomb in which his body was laid, linen wraps and all.

In raising Lazarus, Jesus was giving us a picture of our future. The hope we have as Christians is not some phantom-like existence after death or reincarnation. Our hope is in the resurrection of ourselves, only without the sickness or limitations that currently afflict our physical bodies (Philippians 3:21). Like Lazarus, we will be ourselves. The only difference is that Lazarus had to suffer physical death again, but at our resurrection we will live forever (John 5:28-29).

John says that "many of the Jews therefore, who had come with Mary and had seen what he did, believed in him"

(v. 45; cf. 12:11). Their faith was right on target. Martha's shortsighted view of Jesus as inferior prophet came apart at the seams. Mary's doubts about Jesus' compassion melted and were replaced with even more love and trust. Jesus had made a bold claim that He was the resurrection and the life. Now because He had raised Lazarus from the dead, there could be no doubt that His claims were true. Unfortunately, not even a resurrection convinces those whose hearts are set against God and close to the truth. The Pharisees would not believe, but it wasn't for lack of evidence.

Discussion

1. Why is it easier to build something from scratch than to remodel?

2. What kind of world has the Great Commission sent us into?

3. Why was Bethany an important place to Jesus?

4. How long did Jesus delay visiting Bethany after He heard that Lazarus was sick? Why did He wait?

5. What was Martha's understanding about who Jesus was?

6. What is the significance of the "I am" statements of Jesus in the book of John?

7. What is the Good Confession?

8. What was Mary's understanding about who Jesus was?

9. Describe Jesus' emotional state at the tomb of Lazarus. Why was He upset?

10. What does Lazarus' resurrection teach us about the resurrection that awaits us?

TEN

THE INSPIRATION OF THE BIBLE

"The Bible will give Christ to you in an intimacy so close that he would be less visible to you if he stood before your eyes."

-Erasmus

In the beginning God planted faith into people's hearts through miracles. But after miracles served their purpose, they had to be replaced by a more permanent source of faith: *the Word of God.* Paul writes that "faith comes from hearing, and hearing through the word of Christ" (Romans 10:17). Today we do not believe because we have personally experienced water being turned into wine or a paralyzed person suddenly gaining the ability to wiggle his toes. Now that those events are in the history books, we believe because of testimony. The Bible contains information God wants us to believe, and we have faith when we read it and accept it.

But why should we believe the Bible? In his book, *Mere Christianity*, C.S. Lewis gave his famous "trilemma" argument to discourage people from taking the position that Jesus may have been a good teacher, but He was not the Son of God:

> I am trying here to prevent anyone saying the really foolish thing that people often say about Him: 'I'm ready to accept Jesus as a great moral teacher, but I

don't accept His claim to be God.' That is the one thing we must not say. A man who was merely a man and said the sort of things Jesus said would not be a great moral teacher. He would either be a lunatic—on a level with the man who says he is a poached egg—or else he would be the Devil of Hell. You must make your choice. Either this man was, and is, the Son of God: or else a madman or something worse. You can shut Him up for a fool, you can spit at Him and kill Him as a demon; or you can fall at His feet and call Him Lord and God. But let us not come with any patronizing nonsense about His being a great human teacher. He has not left that open to us. He did not intend to.[1]

Lewis's point was that we cannot simply say Jesus was a good teacher and leave it at that. Jesus did not give us the option. Because He claimed to be the Son of God, we have only three options to choose from: He was a lunatic, a liar, or He really was the Lord.

We are faced with the same trilemma when we approach the Bible. The Bible does not leave open to us the possibility that it is just another good book because of the claims that it makes. For example, in 2 Timothy 3:16-17, Paul writes, "All Scripture is breathed out by God and profitable for teaching, for reproof, for correction, and for training in righteousness, that the man of God may be competent, equipped for every good work." The Bible says it has been "breathed out by God" (other translations use the word "inspired"). The Greek word translated "breathed out" here is a compound word formed from *theos*, meaning "God" and *pneuma*, meaning "breath" or "spirit." The word literally means "God-breathed." Your breath comes from deep inside of you and cannot be detected by the eyes (although unfortunately it can sometimes be detected by the nose!). In the same way, the Bible says that it has come from deep within God, from His Spirit, and has invisibly made its way to our hearts. That is a bold claim!

Peter says this in 2 Peter 1:20-21: "...no prophecy of Scripture comes from someone's own interpretation. For no prophecy was ever produced by the will of man, but men spoke from God as they were carried along by the Holy Spirit." Scripture, Peter says, did not come from the imaginations of the human authors. These authors were miraculously "carried along by the Holy Spirit" as they wrote.

These claims leave us with only three options: either the Bible was penned by lunatics who sincerely thought they were prophets but were writing under a delusion; or it was written by liars who knew they were deceiving the world; or it was composed according to its claims and really is the Word of God.

Before we draw conclusions on which of these three options is most reasonable, let's investigate the claims of the Bible further. What do they actually mean?

Verbal

There are very few explanations in the Bible about how inspiration worked. The lengthiest is probably found in Paul's first letter to the Corinthians. Speaking of the instruction he had been sharing with the Corinthians through preaching and writing, Paul says,

> These things God has revealed to us through the Spirit. For the Spirit searches everything, even the depths of God. For who knows a person's thoughts

except the spirit of that person, which is in him? So also no one comprehends the thoughts of God except the Spirit of God. Now we have received not the spirit of the world, but the Spirit who is from God, that we might understand the things freely given us by God. And we impart this in words not taught by human wisdom but taught by the Spirit, interpreting spiritual truths to those who are spiritual. (1 Corinthians 2:10-13)

Paul says that he and the other apostles got their message miraculously through the Holy Spirit. The Spirit is the right person for the job of revealing God's heart, for He "searches everything, even the depths of God" (v. 10). Paul elaborates on the Spirit's role using a helpful analogy: "For who knows a person's thoughts except the spirit of that person, which is in him? So also no one comprehends the thoughts of God except the Spirit of God" (v. 11). I cannot know what you are thinking as you are reading this book, whether you are reading it intently, suffering from boredom, or disagreeing with it. I will never know unless you tell me, and even then you could be deceiving me. Your thoughts are private, maybe the last privacy you have. In George Orwell's terrifying political novel *1984*, a totalitarian government employs "Thought Police" to punish "thoughtcrime"—thoughts disapproved by the government. But even in Orwell's imaginative novel, the Thought Police did not have the power to peer directly into the characters' minds. They employed surveillance cameras, psychology, and even children to uncover it, but as long as the characters kept their thoughts to themselves, they remained private.

If it is impossible to crack the thoughts of a human being, how will we ever plumb the depths of God? Paul answers, "The Spirit can tell us God's heart because the Spirit and the Father are one. He comprehends the thoughts of God and communicates them to man."

It is to our advantage that the Spirit revealed God's will in "words." The name for this is "verbal inspiration." What if the Spirit had only revealed God's thoughts to the human authors? How reliable would their writings be? The thoughts within them would have been perfect because they came from God, but as the authors translated these thoughts into words, they would have eventually made mistakes because they were human, and humans always make mistakes. If the Spirit had given us only God's thoughts, our faith could not have been certain. But Paul says, "We impart this in *words* not taught by human wisdom but taught by the Spirit" (emphasis mine). The claim is that every word originally penned by the inspired writers of the Bible came miraculously through the Spirit.

Miraculous

How does inspiration work? Some have theorized that the Bible is the product of natural genius – that by providence God endowed the writers with powerful intellects just as he did Shakespeare and Dostoevsky. If that is all that the Bible claims, then it deserves no more honor than *Hamlet* or *The Brothers Karamazov*. Those are great works, but they do not deserve the honor of a book from God.

On the other end of the spectrum, some imagine that the authors of the Bible were nothing more than God's typewriters. Maybe they went into a trance, and God took over their hands to write His Word. Maybe they woke up from a nap to find a finished manuscript without knowing how it came into being! This is an interesting theory, but it cannot explain why the book of the Bible are written in different styles and in different languages. Paul's letters do not read like David's poetry, and Moses' law is very different from Luke's history. If God produced the Bible through its writers while they were unconscious, that would not explain these differences.

So how did the process of inspiration work? Norman Geisler and William Nix give this explanation in their *General Introduction to the Bible*:

> Inspiration is that mysterious process by which the divine causality [i.e., God, D.K.] worked through the human prophets without destroying their individual personalities and styles to produce divinely authoritative and inerrant writings.[2]

Because of the limitations of our minds, the process of inspiration remains a mystery to us. Inspiration was just as much a miracle as Jesus' walking on the water. We cannot understand it, but we can know what has been revealed about it: that God revealed His Word to the human authors in words so that we can know His will for our lives.

Complete

Another common misunderstanding about the Bible is that it merely contains the Word of God, that parts of it are inspired, but that much of it is nothing more than human invention. For example, it is fashionable to read Paul's instructions regarding male spiritual leadership in 1 Timothy 2:11-12 as cultural, even though Paul clearly reaches beyond culture to creation as the basis for his instructions. How do we exclude this passage without limiting inspiration to parts of the Bible instead of the whole? And if only parts are inspired, who gets to select which parts are from God and which are from man? A person would have to be very bold to put himself in the position of deciding for the human race which parts of the Bible God means for us to follow today.

In 2 Timothy 3:16, Paul said "all Scripture" was breathed out by God, not some. The same passage that claims inspiration claims that God inspired every part of the Bible—the poetry, law, history, letters, and prophecy. The historical parts are just as much the Word of God as the doctrinal parts. We cannot pick and choose which parts of the Bible we believe to be from God. According to the Bible's claims, it is either all or nothing.

Accurate

Think for a moment about the impact of what we have learned. What if we really had a book from God? It would have to be perfect. It could not make a single mistake when it mentioned historical places, dates, scientific matters, or other details, and it could not contain a single contradiction. The Bible really sticks its neck out when it claims to be inspired because one mistake disproves its claims. If the Bible is not completely accurate, it cannot be the work of an omniscient, perfect God.

It is important to point out that these claims were made about the original writings of the inspired writers, not the copies or the translations that have been passed down. If a skeptic finds a minor transmission error or an inaccurate translation, that does not discredit the Bible's claims. Those claims have to do only with the originals. It is unfair to hold them up against something less than that.

When we examine the Bible for the marks of inspiration, what do we find? First of all, we notice its remarkable unity. Even though the Bible was written by at least forty different authors over a time period of 1,600 years, not one legitimate contradiction has ever been found within its pages. Now, you can go online and find hundreds of lists of supposed "Bible contradictions," but if you take the time to examine each alleged contradiction, you will find that every example can be explained in a way that preserves the Bible's unity. Everyone can agree that the Bible is a respected book with an impressive amount of evidence backing up its authenticity. It at least deserves the consideration given other books of antiquity. When a contradiction is charged, the burden of proof rests on the skeptic making the charge, not on the believer. If we can present a plausible explanation for the supposed contradiction, that should be enough to satisfy the question. There is no need to back up every historical detail with archaeological evidence that may not yet exist.

Another characteristic of the Bible that makes it stand out from other books of antiquity is its factual accuracy. Whenever it mentions historical or scientific details, it never makes a mistake. For example, scholar Norman Geisler says that archaeology has confirmed not dozens, but hundreds and hundreds of details from the biblical account of the early church.[3] Throughout the years, one skeptic after another has been embarrassed because he mocked historical details in the Bible that were later corroborated by archaeological evidence. Factual inaccuracy in a book this old, or any book for that matter, would be impossible if it had not come from God.

One final evidence of inspiration worth mentioning is predictive prophecy. There are hundreds of prophecies regarding the Messiah in the Old Testament that were fulfilled by Jesus hundreds of years later. These prophecies contain remarkable details, so they cannot be explained away because of their ambiguity. Hundreds of years before the life of Christ, the prophets predicted that He would be born in Bethlehem (Micah 5:2) of a virgin (Isaiah 7:14), that His hands and feet would be pierced (Psalm 22:16) and that soldiers would cast lots for His garments (Psalm 22:18). Isaiah 53 predicted the purpose for His death in amazing detail, reading like one of Paul's theological explanations of the substitutionary nature of the cross. And Daniel was able to pinpoint the time of the coming of the kingdom of Christ in Daniel 2 and 9. How could these prophets know so much so many years ahead of time? The only reasonable conclusion is that God in His omniscience revealed these details to them to confirm His Son when He came.

After examining all of these claims and the evidence backing them up, what should we conclude about the Bible? Is it just another book? It does not leave us with that option, since it claims to be the very breath of God. Is the work of lunatics? One could hardly accept that a book this influential and accurate could be the product of people suffering from delusions. Could it be the work of liars? If so, what was their motive? Most of the biblical authors died for what they wrote. They lived penniless, roving from place to place with their enemies in hot pursuit. Not only that, but how could so many liars keep their story straight? Deceit does not seem to be behind the Bible's writing. Is it possible that the Bible is exactly what it claims to be, the Word of God? That is the inescapable conclusion we are left with after examining the evidence.

If the Bible is really God's Word, we must accept it as the highest authority over our lives. How can we ignore its demands and not believe its warnings and promises? The Bible's testimony is just as powerful in producing faith as the miracles we read about in its pages. As long as the Bible is read, faith will continue to grow in people's hearts.

Discussion

1. Now that the miraculous age has passed, how does God plant faith in our hearts today?

2. What "trilemma" do we face as we approach the Bible?

3. What does "inspiration" mean?

4. What does it mean to say that the inspiration of the Bible is "verbal"?

5. Do we know exactly how the process of inspiration worked? What do we know?

6. How much of the Bible is inspired? Can we pick and choose which parts we believe to be from God?

7. Can the Bible be inspired without being completely accurate? Why or why not?

8. How many inspired authors wrote the Bible? Why is this impressive?

9. Give some examples of predictive prophecy in the Bible.

10. Could the Bible have been written by lunatics or deceivers, or was it written by inspired men?

ELEVEN

HOW TO STUDY THE BIBLE

"Our whole dignity consists in thinking."
-Blaise Pascal

The inspired Scriptures are God's way of conferring faith upon believers today. "Faith comes from hearing," Paul says, "and hearing through the word of Christ" (Romans 10:17). How do inspired words on a page transform into abiding trust in the heart? "Hearing," the apostle says. He doesn't mean detecting sounds with your ears. By "hearing," Paul means learning the Word of God through the effort of study. When Jesus told parables, He would say, "He who has ears, let him hear" (Matthew 13:9). What did He mean? Everybody has ears. Jesus meant that His parables would help only those who put forth enough effort to open their ears, listen, and learn. The Bible is not going to benefit anybody unless he studies it.

The world needs to hear the Word of God so that faith can grow in the hearts of those who listen. What kind of effort is required for someone to study the Bible? Here are some helpful tips.

Make Study a Priority

Bible study should be a priority in your life for many reasons. First of all, without the Bible, there can be no faith, and without faith, there can be no salvation (John 8:24; Acts 16:30-31; Romans 10:9-10; Ephesians 2:8-9). This is why some passages speak of salvation coming through the Word of God (James 1:21; Ephesians 1:13). Ultimately, we are saved by the blood of Jesus Christ, but we cannot know this without the Bible (Romans 10:14).

Bible study is also a source of comfort in the life of the Christian. It is hard to imagine how people without the hope of the gospel are able to go on. Paul said, "For whatever was written in former days was written for our instruction, that through endurance and through the encouragement of the Scriptures we might have hope" (Romans 15:4). The inspired authors of the Bible are the best "counselors" in the world! (Psalm 119:24).

The Bible also gives our lives meaning. God's Word reveals that we were created for holy things, not worldly pursuits and that our highest satisfaction is found in our Creator (Ecclesiastes 3:11; Isaiah 43:7; Acts 17:26-28).

The most common excuse for not studying the Bible is, "I just don't have enough time!" If you don't have time, move something around, and make time! We can find time to do those things that are most important to us. What is keeping us from Bible study? Television? Video games? Facebook? Ball games? Reading? Phone calls? Visiting with friends? Golf? We may have to eliminate some things to make room for study. Lin Yutang said, "Besides the noble art of getting things done, there is the noble art of leaving things undone. The wisdom of life consists of the elimination of nonessentials."[1] People who study their Bibles have no more time in their lives than anybody else. Most of them are very busy people. They have made Bible study a priority.

Focus on a Plan

The difference between casual reading and study is a plan. Your plan may be as general as the one Paul gave Timothy in 2 Timothy 2:15: "Do your best ["study," KJV] to present yourself to God as one approved, a worker who has no need to be ashamed, rightly handling the word of truth." Timothy's work involved teaching the "word of truth." This requires diligent study. Paul did not want Timothy to be "ashamed," so he gave him a study plan to present himself to God "as one approved," who "rightly handles the word of truth."

Your plan might be to figure out a difficult theological question, or read through the Bible in a year, or teach a series of lessons, or memorize a section of Scripture, or prepare yourself to answer questions regarding a number of topics. There are hundreds of good Bible study plans to choose from. Pick one and focus on it. Without a plan, we wind up wandering through the Scriptures aimlessly and getting nowhere.

Study

What does it mean to "study" the Bible? What activities are involved?

Reading

"Real reading," author Wendell Berry says, "is a kind of work. But it's lovely work."[2] If that is true of reading all books in general, think of how much lovelier it is to read the Word of God!

Are we reading the Bible as if it were "lovely work"? Are we reading it at all? Sadly, while Americans revere the Bible, they don't read it.[3] A LifeWay Research study reports that only 45 percent of those who regularly attend church read the Bible more than once a week. Over 40 percent of the people attending read their Bible occasionally, maybe once or twice a month. And almost one in five churchgoers say they never read the Bible at all![4]

When you do the math, the time that it takes to read the Old Testament comes to about fifty-two hours, and it takes another eighteen hours to read the New Testament. Do we have seventy hours a year to read God's Word? Surely, we can find the time!

Thinking

John Piper defines "thinking" as reading and understanding the Bible.[5] So when you are reading the Bible, the words should be penetrating more deeply than your eyes. You should be thinking about what you are reading.

Asking questions is a helpful way to promote thinking. For example, read Jesus' statement in Matthew 7:12: "So whatever you wish that others would do to you, do also to them, for this is the Law and the Prophets." Now, ask yourself:

- What is it that I wish others would do for me?
- Am I willing to do the same for them?
- Why am I reluctant to do things for others when I would like them to do those things for me?
- What does Jesus mean by "the Law and the Prophets"? How does this rule sum them up?

Questions breed thoughts, and thinking is at the heart of study.

Memorizing

There are many good reasons why a Christian should devote time to the memorization of Scripture. The new covenant is meant to be a relationship with God in which

He puts His laws into the hearts and the minds of His people (Hebrews 8:10). Christians are to be people of the book. As we have said, reading the Bible is a profitable and necessary discipline, but memorization deepens the understanding. If you are struggling to understand a passage of Scripture, try committing it to memory. You will discover important connections, wordings, and subtle references you never would have caught by simply reading the text. Furthermore, memorization guards us against temptations to sin. The psalmist said, "I have stored up your word in my heart, that I might not sin against you" (119:11). What did Jesus do when He was tempted by the devil in the wilderness? He met every temptation with a memorized Scripture prefaced by the phrase "it is written" (Matthew 4:4, 7, 10). The practice of memorizing Scripture can be very satisfying. We fill our minds with so many worldly things. Why not fill them with words that foster life? (John 6:68).

Praying

Prayer is the act of continuing a conversation initiated by God in Scripture.[6] Paul instructs us to "pray without ceasing" (1 Thessalonians 5:17). Therefore, our lives should be an ongoing conversation in which the Father speaks to us through His Word, and we respond through prayer.

When Martin Luther meditated upon a passage of Scripture, he divided it into four parts:

- Instruction – What does the Lord demand of me?
- Thanksgiving – How does this teaching lead me to praise and thank God?
- Confession – How does it lead me to repent and confess sin?

- Prayer – How does it prompt me to appeal to God in petition and supplication?[7]

Without prayer, Bible study is a one-sided conversation. God wants a relationship with us, and in relationships, both sides communicate in loving conversation. Prayer, then, is essential to the completion of our studies.

Pay Attention to the Context

It is possible to support just about any teaching with the Bible by taking passages out of context. When we speak of the "context" of a Bible passage, we are talking about the information before and after a passage of Scripture. The *specific* context of the passage has to do with, say, the paragraphs prior to and following the passage. The *general* context may have to do with the whole chapter, the book, the testament, or the Bible.

Considering the context means asking who is speaking and what are the circumstances in which the words were written. Also, context ensures that our interpretation does not contradict other passages of Scripture on the same subject. If we arrive at a conclusion that is in clear contradiction to another Bible passage, we must revisit our interpretation.

After Jesus' resurrection, He encountered two disciples who were on their way to the village of Emmaus, about seven miles outside of Jerusalem (Luke 24:13-15). Strangely, they did not recognize their Lord and talked with Him about the events that had transpired in Jerusalem over the previous few days (v. 16). Over the course of this unusual conversation, Jesus decided to correct some of their mistaken impressions concerning His mission and purpose. Luke tells us, "And beginning with Moses and all the

Prophets, he interpreted to them in all the Scriptures the things concerning himself" (v. 27). Jesus did not conduct His study piecemeal, pulling from one proof-text here and another there in order to make His points. Rather, "beginning with Moses and all the Prophets," He led His disciples through a systematic examination of the Scriptures. God's Word becomes a dangerous tool in the hands of a person who has no respect for the context. Satan himself has twisted the Scriptures to his own purposes (Matthew 4:6; cf. 2 Peter 3:15-16).

Get Some Good Tools

Paul called Timothy a "workman" or "laborer" (2 Timothy 2:15). Every laborer has trustworthy tools that help him do his job. Bible study is no different. You will need a good library that includes dictionaries on biblical words, reputable commentaries, various translations, concordances, topical studies, works on Apologetics, works of literature, philosophy, and resources for historical background. We are fortunate to live in an age in which many of these resources are available free on the Internet. Always be careful, however, where you go for your information. Many websites can be misleading.[8]

Start a Routine

You will have to manage your time in order to work the study of the Bible into your busy schedule. For this reason, start a routine in which you have already decided on a time and a place for your Bible study.

Choose a time when you will not be bothered by distractions and when your mind is fresh and able to work. You may have to get up early. Some people's minds are fresher in the morning. Also, if you study first thing in the morning, you are less likely to run into interferences. If you are not an earlybird, you may choose to stay up late. Some parents wait until the kids are in bed before they turn to their studies so that their reading and thinking can be free of distractions. Just know that the later you wait in the day to do your studies, the easier it is to make excuses. You will get tired, or there will be interruptions. If it is possible, earlier is better.

Choose a place that is well-lit and free of distractions. Don't study in front of the television or in a room full of people. Put your phone on silent and keep it out of sight. Have your study tools nearby and arrange things so that you are seated comfortably in front of a desk. It is important that these arrangements be the same every time. You are trying to establish a routine. Despite preaching forty meetings a year, Guy N. Woods was able to establish a routine he could follow no matter where he was. Wherever he went, he carried a fold-up desk and a typewriter that he would set up when he arrived for his speaking appointment. Whether he was in a hotel or staying in someone's home, he would arrange all the furniture in the room, within reason, so that nothing would distract him. He claimed this was the best way for him to work.[9] Woods wrote articles, edited papers, typed up lectures, and finished lengthy commentaries while traveling most of the year, because he followed a routine.

In the age of miracles, it may have been possible for someone to receive faith passively, although in many cases witnesses to miracles walked away unchanged in their unbelief. Now that God conveys faith through His Word, more effort is required for belief to take root in our hearts. If we do not study the Bible, we will not believe. "He who has ears, let him hear."

Discussion

1. What does Paul mean by "hearing" in Romans 10:17?

2. In what sense does salvation come through the Word of God?

3. How can we make more time for Bible study?

4. What makes the difference between casual reading and study?

5. How long on average does it take to read the Bible?

6. How do you promote thinking while reading the Bible?

7. What are some reasons why Christians should memorize Scripture?

8. Why is prayer essential to the completion of our studies?

9. What is context? Why is it so important to the understanding of God's Word?

10. What are some good tools you can invest in to aid your Bible study?

TWELVE

OBEDIENCE THROUGH SUFFERING

"Suffering is the climate in which a man's soul begins to breathe."

-Soren Kierkegaard

God plants faith in the hearts of believers as farmers plant seed in the soil. He does it painstakingly because the stakes are high. Without faith there is no eternal life.

Today, faith comes through hearing the Word of Christ (Romans 10:17), but we are not to misunderstand "hearing" to mean simply listening to the words of the Bible. Jesus said that would be following in the steps of the fool who built his house upon sand (Matthew 7:24-27). James concurred, saying, "But be doers of the word, and not hearers only, deceiving yourselves" (James 1:22).

We have discussed the inspired nature of God's faith-delivery system, the Bible, how it is infallible and trustworthy. The Holy Spirit may not miraculously reveal God's Word any longer,[1] but He has insured that it has been written down so that we may read it and understand God's will for our lives (Ephesians 3:4). When we do that, we may be surprised to find that God's Word is often very challenging and that to acquire the kind of faith that saves, the believer must sometimes suffer to obey God.

Hebrews 5 provides us with an excellent model of how to learn obedience through suffering by giving us a picture of the crucifixion from heaven's perspective. How do you picture the crucifixion? There are numerous viewpoints. The earliest extant picture of a crucifixion mocks Christianity by picturing an individual praying to a figure with the head of a donkey on a cross.[2] On the other end of the spectrum, the Renaissance painter Paolo Veronese pictures Jesus hanging twenty feet in the air, His pierced side bleeding, and His mother Mary swooning below with grief. The French painter James Tissot painted the scene of the crucifixion from the vantage point of the cross, looking down at expressions of pride, stoicism, and grief. We imagine the cross in beautiful hymns, such as, "When I Survey the Wondrous Cross," in which we sing,

> See from His head, His hands, His feet,
> Sorrow and love flow mingled down!
> Did e'er such love and sorrow meet,
> Or thorns compose so rich a crown?[3]

To the Romans, Jesus' death was one in thousands, the death of an unknown criminal from Galilee. To the Jews, it was the justified execution of a blasphemer. How did the Father regard the death of His Son? Hebrews 5:7-10 reads,

> In the days of his flesh, Jesus offered up prayers and supplications, with loud cries and tears, to him who was able to save him from death, and he was heard because of his reverence. Although he was a son, he learned obedience through what he suffered. And being made perfect, he became the source of eternal salvation to all who obey him, being designated by God a high priest after the order of Melchizedek.

From heaven's perspective, the crucifixion was obedience through suffering. The account from Hebrews 5 works its way up to Calvary by starting where Jesus prepared for this obedience in the Garden of Gethsemane.

The setting was Thursday of the Passover, the eve of our Lord's crucifixion. Jesus' heart was already heavy with grief. He knew one of His disciples would betray Him. He had just risen from His last supper with His closest friends during which time they argued over who was the greatest. The weight of the sins of the world was upon Him, and His darkest hour was approaching.

After supper Jesus and the disciples sang a hymn (Matthew 26:30) and went to the Mount of Olives, across the Kidron Valley from Jerusalem. They turned off into an olive orchard, as its name "Gethsemane" ("oil press") suggests. This was a favorite retreat for Jesus. John says Jesus often met there with His disciples (John 18:2). There are still eight olive trees there. The historian Josephus said Titus destroyed all the olive trees in A.D. 70, so these may not be the trees under which Jesus poured His heart out to his Father.[4] But they are ancient, and a sacred air still surrounds those grounds today.

Gardens have a prominent place in the record of God's dealing with man. The Bible begins with the account of man's fall in the Garden of Eden. It ends with a picture of man enjoying fellowship with God in the Garden of God. Between the Garden of Eden in Genesis and the Garden of God in Revelation there is the Garden of Gethsemane. In this garden the story of how the restoration of fellowship between sinful man and a righteous God came to be is told.

Jesus' distress was evident from the various postures He assumed according to the text. Luke says that He "knelt" (22:41). Mark says He "fell on the ground" (14:35). Matthew says He "fell on his face" (26:39). His emotional condition was also evident from the various words the Holy Spirit used in describing it. The Scriptures say more about the suffering in Gethsemane than they do about the pain Jesus suffered on the cross. Luke says He was in "agony" (22:44). The word that he uses (*agonia*) refers to "consternation, appalled reluctance."[5] Matthew and Mark describe His condition, saying He was "troubled" (Matthew 26:37; Mark 14:33), suggesting "loathing aversion, perhaps not unmixed with despondency."[6] Jesus' own words were, "My soul is very sorrowful, even to death" (Matthew 26:38). Here the word is *perilypos*, which expresses "a mental pain, a distress, which hems him in on every side, from which there is therefore no escape."[7] Mark says He was "deeply distressed" (*ekthambeomai*), which has been rendered "horror-struck"[8] (Mark 14:33). Hebrews records no verbal language but says the Lord's prayers were offered up with "loud cries and tears" (5:7).

Also, there was the physical trauma. Luke tells us, "And being in agony he prayed more earnestly; and his sweat became like great drops of blood falling down to the ground" (22:44). Because of Luke's use of the word "like," the statement is ambiguous and could be read as a simile. It could be that the Lord was sweating so profusely and His agony was so great it was as if the sweat were great drops of blood. However, medical doctors have pointed out that Luke may be referring to a condition called hematidrosis, which occurs in rare cases where intense emotional stress results in blood vessels rupturing into the sweat glands.[9]

Through all of this distress He prayed, "My Father, if it be possible, let this cup pass from me; nevertheless, not as I will, but as you will" (Matthew 26:39). Hebrews 5:7 describes His praying, saying He offered up "prayers and supplications, with loud cries and tears, to him who was able to save him from death" (Heb. 5:7). Was He afraid to die? It does sound like He was trying to escape death. This idea may be plausible from a human vantage point, especially when the death of crucifixion is considered. However, it is too simple an explanation to say that the prospect of dying on a cross caused Jesus this level of mental anguish. His knowledge of the afterlife and the moral courage He showed throughout His ministry cannot support such a conclusion. Socrates, according to Plato's account, took his cup of hemlock without trembling or changing color or expression. Was he braver than Jesus?

We must understand that no death comes remotely close to Jesus' death.[10] In this "hour" Jesus was preparing for in the Garden, He carried our sins to the cross, He was despised by those for whom He was making such a sacrifice, and the Father's face turned away from His only Son (Matthew 27:46). His agony was depicted in His prayers as a "cup," a common symbol for His wrath (Job 21:20; Ezekiel 23:32-34).[11] Therefore, the "cup" Jesus sought to avoid was the agony of enduring divine judgment over the sins He had to bear.

The human suffering of the Son of God might seem to be an unusual detail for the inspired writers to include in the gospel. Jesus is Lord. He will judge the world when He returns (Acts 17:31). Is it really necessary for us to read about his "loud cries and tears"? Actually, it is. The bleeding, crying, thirsting, and anguish is all there to teach us two very important lessons about obedience.

The Reason for Obedience

The general lack of commitment among professing Christians in the U.S. is well documented. According to the

Barna Research Group, 73 percent of Americans say they are Christian, but only 31 percent attend a church service at least once a month. About the same percentage say that they read their Bible regularly. The numbers are lower when it comes to service. Only 18 percent in the U.S. volunteer to serve at a church or nonprofit organization.[12]

One of the reasons for this large discrepancy between those who call themselves Christian and those who practice Christianity is the oversimplification of what it means to be a follower of Christ. It would seem that following Christ can be summed up as being "forgiven." The rest is icing on the cake. Modern Christianity's low involvement in the church comes from the attitude that says, "Jesus died so that I do not have to worry about my sin. Whether I follow him beyond conversion is entirely up to me." Dallas Willard gives this attitude the name "barcode" Christianity. Professing Christians today are satisfied with being read by the "great scanner in the sky" as possessing eternal life. They have reduced the Christian life to merely receiving forgiveness. This has made obedience to Jesus in daily life irrelevant.[13]

If the reason for obedience is only to receive forgiveness, why did Jesus obey the Father? He had no sin to be forgiven. Jesus may have died for sins, but they were not His sins. Hebrews 4:15 reads, "For we do not have a high priest who is unable to sympathize with our weaknesses, but one who in every respect has been tempted as we are, yet without sin." Describing Jesus' demeanor on the cross, Peter explained, "He committed no sin..." (1 Peter 2:22). Whatever the reason for His willingness to obey God all the way to Calvary, it was not penance for sin.

Had Jesus remained in heaven, He would have continued to enjoy the glories there (Philippians 2:5-8). He was not forced to die on the cross. One command would have summoned angels from every corner of heaven to His aid (Matthew 26:53). He told His disciples,

> For this reason the Father loves me, because I lay down my life that I may take it up again. No one takes it from me, but I lay it down of my own accord. I have authority to lay it down, and I have authority to take it up again. This charge I have received from my Father. (John 10:17-18)

Jesus must have obeyed the Father for reasons other than forgiveness.

Jesus desired what His Father desired, in this case the salvation of the human race. Jesus' desire was to be made "perfect," and perfection was achieved because of His obedience. Of course, He was already morally perfect. But His role as high priest and Savior could not have been completed until His death. This is the context of Hebrews 5:7-10. The author has been listing six essential qualifications required for Jesus to become our high priest. Raymond Brown lists them as follows:

- He had to be appointed by God (Hebrews 5:5).
- He had to be identified with men (Hebrews 2:17-18).
- He had to be sensitive to human need (Hebrews 4:15).
- He had to be victorious over sin (Hebrews 4:15).
- He had to be obedient to the divine purpose (Hebrews 5:8).
- He had to be willing to die to affect man's deliverance (Hebrews 2:14).[14]

Because He allowed God to perfect Him, Jesus "became the source of eternal salvation to all who obey him" (Hebrews 5:9). This was what was on His mind, not simply a selfish desire to be free of annoying guilt.

When we find a reason to obey that includes forgiveness, but embraces more of God's will for our lives, we are preparing ourselves for heaven. Ultimately heaven is living with God (Revelation 21:3, 22-24; 22:1-5). Christ calls us to begin that experience now as we seek obedience to His Word.

The Education of Obedience
What did the writer of Hebrews mean when he said Jesus "learned obedience through what he suffered"? (Hebrews 5:8). Did he mean that Jesus needed to learn something intellectually? This cannot be the correct interpretation. Jesus, being divine, knows everything. He is omniscient. He cannot learn anything or forget anything.

Did he mean that Jesus had been rebellious and finally got his act together? Of course, this is absurd. Jesus is as infinitely righteous as He is knowing. He has never rebelled against heaven. Even when He was a child, Jesus was submissive in every way (Luke 2:51).

Jesus' learning obedience refers to the *experience* of obedience. Before He left heaven to live as a young man on earth, Jesus never suffered temptation the way that He did in Gethsemane. In the garden, with His face buried in the sacred soil, tears streaming down His cheeks, He experienced a new kind of obedience, one that led to immense suffering. The difference between Jesus in heaven and Jesus' learning obedience on earth is the difference between innocence and experience. Innocence is life untested, but experience is life tested and successfully conquered.

People rationalize sin saying, "Obedience is harder for me than others. Life is not as easy for me as it was for Christ or as it is for other people who are obedient." But it is precisely when obedience is hard that it is made real. This is the only sense in which Jesus could have learned obedience through suffering. He had to come to earth where obedience is hard to experience it.

Unlike Jesus, we have much to learn in terms of information *and* experience, and that may be the secret to the reason God's children have to suffer. We get information through God's Word, but while the Bible gives us the *how* and *why* of obedience, it does not supply the *what*. We must learn the experience of obedience through suffering. This is described as "discipline" later in Hebrews:

> And have you forgotten the exhortation that addresses you as sons? "My son, do not regard lightly the discipline of the Lord, nor be weary when reproved by him. For the Lord disciplines the one he loves, and chastises every son whom he receives." It is for discipline that you have to endure. God is treating you as sons. (Hebrews 12:5-7)

Although he was not a religious man, the poet John Keats, who died at the age of 25, may have arrived at the same conclusion. In a letter written on April 21, 1819 to his brother, George, who had emigrated to America, Keats unveiled a theory that he'd been designing and testing for more than a year: the world as the "vale of Soul-making." Keats referred to the raw material of a soul as an "intelligence." All humans have an intelligence, but they're not considered souls until they develop an individual identity. Soul creation takes place over the span of many years and requires two components—the human heart and the world of feverish suffering—comprising a process that Keats likened to an education: "Do you not see how necessary a World of Pains and troubles is to school an Intelligence and make it a soul? A Place where the heart must feel and suffer in a thousand diverse ways!"[15] Keats was onto something. This world is a school room of eternity. The present life determines our destiny. After this life, our eternal destination is set in stone (cf. Luke 16:26).

Naturally, we would all prefer to remain as ignorant infants in our mother's arms, having every need met by somebody else and never having to hurt or worry about anything. God has something far greater in store for us. He sent His Son to the cross to die for our spiritual redemption, to be followed by a complete redemption at the end of time (Romans 8:23). His will for us is far better than anything we could imagine for ourselves. Do we trust Him enough to obey His commands, even when they challenge us and lead us towards hardship? Look to Jesus' example. Learn obedience with Him and let your faith flourish as you grow.

Discussion

1. What are some different perspectives on the cross? What is God's point of view?

2. Where did Jesus prepare for His obedience at Calvary?

3. Was Jesus' emotional state evident in the Garden of Gethsemane? How so?

4. Was Jesus afraid to die? If not, how do we explain His agony in the Garden?

5. Why is there a discrepancy between those who call themselves Christians and those who practice Christianity?

6. Was Jesus forced to die on the cross?

7. In what sense was Jesus made perfect through His obedience?

8. What does the Bible mean when it says Jesus "learned" obedience?

9. Why is discipline important?

10. Explain the phrase "vale of Soul-making."

THIRTEEN

PLANTING FAITH

"We heed, O Lord, Thy summons,
And answer: Here are we!
Send us upon Thine errand,
Let us Thy servants be.
Our strength is dust and ashes,
Our years a passing hour;
But Thou canst use our weakness
To magnify Thy power."

-John Haynes Holmes

We have spent most of our time discussing the pursuit of faith. Now let's examine how faith blossoms from the opposite end, from the point of view of the people who are actively trying to spread their faith through evangelism.

We live in a very difficult time for evangelism. We can attribute much of the trouble to changing attitudes towards belief in God. In the past, it was unthinkable for an individual to publicly declare that he or she does not believe in God, but now atheism has become socially acceptable. One church leader who works in a community where the skeptics make up a large demographic shares,

> In my experience…unchurched people think the Bible and the gospel are cultural artifacts that are no longer relevant. The unchurched audience is rejecting the church for worldview issues….The

bottom line is we evangelicals are answering questions no one is asking.[1]

In other words, Christians are out of touch with skeptics. We are saying, "The Bible is right; sin is wrong; these religions are wrong." And they are asking, "Why are these people subjecting me to their way of thinking? Why won't they leave me alone? I'm not hurting anybody." All the while, nobody is saying much about Jesus.

To overcome the gap between our worldview and the world's, we must ask a question that interests everyone regardless of his background. The question is similar to the one Jesus asked His disciples in Matthew 16:15: "Who do you say that I am?" Jesus is a subject that still interests everyone. Some are antagonistic towards Him, some love Him, some make Him the center of their lives, and some are puzzled by Him, but everyone has an opinion about Him. If we are going to plant our faith in unbelievers today, we must get them talking about Jesus: "What do you think about Jesus? Do you think that He actually lived, or do you believe that He is a myth? What do you think about His teachings? Do you believe that He rose from the dead? Is it possible that we can know whether a carpenter from Nazareth really walked the earth 2,000 years ago?" Jesus will get the conversation going rather than bring the door slamming hard into our faces.

An example of the kind of conversation I am talking about is found in John 4, where Jesus speaks with a Samaritan woman at Jacob's well. Jesus' conversation with the Samaritan woman is an interesting case for several reasons. First of all, Jesus is in a place where He shouldn't be, speaking with a person He shouldn't talk to according to the customs of His day. Also, the conversation He has with the woman is essentially a case of Christ preaching Christ. He is both the subject and the object of His own lesson. What's more, He does as much listening as He does talking. This is an actual conversation, not a lecture. When we study this conversation, we have the privilege of watching the Master Sower at work. If we followed His example, our fumbling attempts at evangelism would not be so unsuccessful.

What He Did
John tells us that Jesus "had to pass through Samaria" (v. 4). This is a strange statement, because He was on His way from Judea to Galilee, and the customary route taken by the Jews would have been to cross the Jordan River going east, travel north through Perea, and cross the Jordan into Galilee after going far enough north to bypass Samaria. As John put it, Jews had no dealings with Samaritans (v. 9). In fact there was great hatred on the part of both ethnic groups because of a history filled with war, captivity, and a disruption in the cherished bloodline of Abraham.

The Samaritan race probably originated with the Assyrian domination of the northern kingdom of Israel in 722 B.C. The Assyrians, who had been successful in numerous military conquests by this time, separated people from their native lands and from their leadership to quell any attempts to revolt against the oppression. Sargon, the king of Assyria at this time, followed this procedure with the Israelites, exiling them to camps in his own land. In their place he settled Samaria, the most affluent district of the northern kingdom, with people from other conquests: Babylon, Cuthah, Avva, Hamath, and Sepharvaim (2 Kings 17:24). More colonists followed under Osnapper (Ezra 4:10). The poorest people of the land, however, were probably left to cultivate the land and make it profitable for Assyria (2 Kings 24:14). The Israelites that remained in Samaria intermarried with those Gentiles who were brought in, and the race of the Samaritans was born.

After the Jews returned from Babylonian captivity in 536 B.C., hatred began to boil between the Samaritans and the "purebred" Jews. This enmity was based partly on the racial differences precipitated by their history, but it was made worse by the Samaritans' construction of a rival temple on Mount Gerizim in Shechem (cf. John 4:20-21).

Disgust was felt on both sides. A Jewish document written in the second century B.C. reads, "Two nations I detest, and the third is no nation at all: the inhabitants of Mount Seir [the Edomites, D.K.], the Philistines, and the senseless folk that live at Shechem [the Samaritans, D.K.]." On the other hand, the Samaritans were capable of fomenting their own rage. On one occasion Jesus and His disciples were traveling from Galilee, through Samaria, to Jerusalem in the south. But one village in Samaria would not allow Jesus to stay there for the night, because "he set His face to go to Jerusalem" (Luke 9:51-53). The Sons of Thunder wanted to call fire from heaven to consume them, but Jesus rebuked them (Luke 9:54-55).

We may think the clash between atheists and Christians is severe in America today, but it approaches nothing like the hatred that boiled between the Jews and the Samaritans. And here is Jesus, making it necessary to pass through that land shunned by His brethren. Why was it necessary for Him to go through Samaria? Was it not because He desired to engage the people there as He had His own people? There could be no other explanation.

It is clear that Jesus was breaking a number of social rules. When He asked the woman for a drink of water, she said, "How is it that you, a Jew, ask for a drink from me, a woman of Samaria?" (v. 9). It should be pointed out that she did not merely point out that she was a Samaritan, but also that she was a woman. It was just as unacceptable for Jesus to be speaking to a woman in public as it was for Him to be speaking with a Samaritan. When His disciples returned from their errands, John says they "marveled" that He was speaking with her, but they dared not say anything about it (v. 27).

What He Taught

Over the course of the conversation Jesus had with the woman, He gradually developed the woman's faith in Him as the Son of God. His natural, easy manner of speaking with her is an example of the type of evangelism that would work for the church today. He did not just talk; He listened to her and allowed her words to become part of the case that He made for Himself as the Messiah. There are three steps taken in this conversation that gradually led to this woman's belief that the Messiah was real and that He was Jesus of Nazareth.

The Giver of Living Water

The two were sitting at Jacob's well, and Jesus had just asked the woman for a drink of water. This is when He began to build her faith by telling her about a different kind of water that only He can give:

> Jesus answered her, "If you knew the gift of God, and who it is that is saying to you, 'Give me a drink,' you would have asked him, and he would have given you living water." The woman said to him, "Sir, you have nothing to draw water with, and the well is deep.

> Where do you get that living water? Are you greater than our father Jacob? He gave us the well and drank from it himself, as did his sons and his livestock." Jesus said to her, "Everyone who drinks of this water will be thirsty again, but whoever drinks of the water that I will give him will never be thirsty again. The water that I will give him will become in him a spring of water welling up to eternal life." The woman said to him, "Sir, give me this water, so that I will not be thirsty or have to come here to draw water." (John 4:10-15)

So far, the woman had no clue who Jesus was. He admitted that He was a mystery: "If you knew...who it is that is saying to you, 'Give me a drink,' you would have asked him, and he would have given you living water" (v. 10). Jesus changed the subject. He was no longer talking about well water but eternal life. Still, the woman did not seem to understand. She knew that He was the giver of living water, but she didn't understand His words in the spiritual sense. She wanted this water so that she would no longer be thirsty or have to draw it out of the well.

The Prophet
Jesus changed the subject again. This time, He was sure to get the woman's attention.

> Jesus said to her, "Go, call your husband, and come here." The woman answered him, "I have no husband." Jesus said to her, "You are right in saying, 'I have no husband'; for you have had five husbands, and the one you now have is not your husband. What

you have said is true." The woman said to him, "Sir, I perceive that you are a prophet." (vv. 16-19).

There are two reasons why Jesus did this. First, adultery is a sin. Until a sinner knows that she is lost, she will not seek the Savior. I know this seems to contradict what I said earlier about the kinds of conversations we need to have with the world, but Jesus wasn't just calling the woman a sinner without knowing her; He described her personal life exactly without having any prior knowledge of her. This wasn't the age of the Internet. He had not been stalking her, and she knew it, which leads to the second reason why He issued this gentle rebuke: He wanted to confirm that He could grant her eternal life. And it worked. The woman was so amazed by His intuition that she declared Him to be a prophet.

The Messiah
They began to speak of their differences. The Samaritans worshiped on Mount Gerazim, but the Jews insisted that God's people should worship in Jerusalem. This conversation led to one of the few ideas the Jews and Samaritans shared. The woman said, "I know that Messiah is coming (he who is called Christ). When he comes, he will tell us all things" (v. 25). That was when Jesus spoke very plainly to her: *I who speak to you am he* (v. 26).

As the woman's words indicate, "Messiah" is the Hebrew equivalent to the Greek "Christ," both meaning "Anointed One." The Samaritans waited with the Jews for this special deliver to come from the Father and bring liberty to their people. It must have been a stunning moment for the woman. We do not know if she was speechless, or if she was about to say something and was interrupted by the disciples when they stumbled upon her conversation with Jesus.

How He Taught

While the disciples distracted Jesus, the woman made a getaway, but she was not trying to escape; she was leaving Jesus so that she could tell her friends about what she had experienced.

Isn't this different than the kind of engagement the church seems to be currently having with the world? There are some successes, but most of the time the world runs away and never returns. Here, the woman ran away so she could bring friends to Jesus. Maybe there is something in her words to the townspeople that gives us a clue about why she was moved in a positive direction.

Her testimony was simple: "Come, see a man who told me all that I ever did. Can this be the Christ?" (v. 29). In those two sentences, we can detect at least three ways in which Jesus affected her.

He made personal contact with her.
This was "a man" who talked to her. In *Churchless*, George Barna and David Kinnaman speak of the ineffectiveness that impersonal evangelistic strategies like social media and direct mailing have on today's culture. Only 18 percent of the unchurched say they would respond to television, radio, or newspaper advertising. The numbers are lower for direct mailings (16 percent) and billboard ads (14 percent).[2] People are lonely. They crave personal engagement. They are looking for someone like Jesus who will stop in the middle of a busy day and just have a conversation with them.

He listened to her.
While a great deal of Jesus' conversation with the woman was about Him, it is amazing how much of it was about her. This impressed her, because her testimony was that He told her "all that she ever did." Jesus listened to her. Somehow, He even taught her by listening. Who was the first person to bring up Jesus' radical disregard for racial prejudice? It was the woman who brought up that He, a Jew, was asking a Samaritan for water (v. 9). This evolved into the Samaritans' exclamation that Jesus was not just the Savior of the Jews, but the "Savior of the world" (v. 42). Who first brought up the woman's sin? Who was the person who called Jesus a prophet? Jesus did not make that claim; the woman perceived that He was a prophet (v. 19). Who first brought up the Messiah? It was the woman (v. 25).

Barna and Kinnaman argue that

> listening, instead of talking, may be the best way to connect with those who don't share Christian worldview assumptions. If we don't take time to hear where skeptics—or any churchless people, for that matter—are coming from and what they are saying, we're not really in a conversation…we're just waiting for our chance to preach.[3]

What if Jesus' conversation with the woman went something like this:

First of all, the worship of the Samaritans has been sinful for years. The temple in Jerusalem is the only authorized place of worship for God's people. Also, before you insert yourself into a religious conversation, you might want to stop committing adultery. Furthermore, you are too concerned about worldly things. Stop worrying about water and how much work it takes you to draw it, and get your mind on spiritual things!

I doubt even the Lord would have gotten very far with this approach. By listening, He communicated everything contained in the lecture above without turning the woman off. Instead of walking off disgusted, she ran to tell her friends that she had found the Christ.

He introduced her to God.
She left asking, "Can this be the Christ?" She did not look upon her conversation with Jesus as another talk with an ordinary rabbi; she believed that she had rubbed shoulders with God. Barna and Kinnaman found through their research that there are two main hurdles between churchless people and deep engagement in churches: 1) the sense that God is missing from church, and 2) the suspicion that Christians are missing the point.[4] It is no wonder why people outside the church feel this way. The religious world is changing churches from places where people come to meet God to houses of entertainment and style where "center stage is empty of the main event."[5] It is not uncommon for the music portion of the assembly to feel more like a performance than a heartfelt offering to God. Preaching has degenerated into feel-good, self-help advice rather than the proclamation of the living Word. A sense of reverence and awe has been replaced with a consumer mentality that seeks the church that can "do worship the best." We are like the disciples—more worried about lunch than the purposes of God.

This is a far cry from the prophet Habakkuk's declaration: "But the Lord is in his holy temple; let all the earth keep silence before him" (2:20).

Jesus' strategy of personal contact, listening, and having the woman experience God worked. He interrupted His disciples' discussion of lunch to tell them, "Look, I tell you, lift up your eyes, and to see that the fields are white for harvest" (verse 35). Contrary to what we might think, Jesus' society was no more responsive than American culture. Religion had become stale, sin ran rampant, and people had lost sight of who God really was. But Jesus knew how to get people to believe. He went to them, listened to them, and showed them God.

Many Samaritans became believers because of Jesus' conversation with the woman. John writes,

> Many Samaritans from that town believed in him because of the woman's testimony, "He told me all that I ever did"....And many more believed because of His word. They said to the woman, "It is no longer because of what you said that we believe, for we have heard for ourselves, and we know that this is indeed the Savior of the world." (John 4:39, 41-42)

It appears that first they believed because of the woman's testimony, but after they met Jesus, they gained a deeper belief by hearing His Word. Their initial belief was legitimate, but it needed to mature. When they were given the opportunity to hear Jesus for themselves, their faith was able to grow. Evangelism must translate testimony into church life. In other words, it is not enough for people to talk about Jesus in the world; they must be assimilated into the body of Christ and begin walking together with brothers and sisters in Christ before their faith will be able to grow in a meaningful way.

Discussion

1. What are some of the special challenges we face in evangelizing the world today?

2. Jesus is still interesting. How do we get people talking about Him?

3. Why is Jesus' conversation with the Samaritan woman an interesting case study?

4. Why did Jesus have to pass through Samaria?

5. Why did the Jews and Samaritans hate one another?

6. Why did Jesus bring up the woman's many husbands?

7. People crave personal engagement. What tempts us away from engaging with people on this level?

8. How can we become better listeners?

9. What are the hurdles between churchless people and deep engagement in churches?

10. After people are converted to Christ, they must be assimilated into the church. How can we get new Christians more involved so that their faith will continue to grow?

APPENDIX

THE HOLY SPIRIT

"These things God has revealed to us through the Spirit. For the Spirit searches everything, even the depths of God."

-1 Corinthians 2:10

The Bible consistently maintains that the Holy Spirit was the agent of miraculous revelation. King David said, "The Spirit of the Lord speaks by me; his word is on my tongue" (2 Samuel 23:2). Paul claimed his preaching came through the Spirit (1 Corinthians 2:10; Ephesians 3:3, 5), and his fellow apostle Peter said, "...men spoke from God as they were carried along by the Holy Spirit" (2 Peter 1:21).

Most believers agree about the Spirit's involvement in the production of the Scriptures. But there is disagreement over the question whether the Spirit continues to be involved in revealing the Word and/or helping Christians understand it. Those who believe the Spirit continues to be involved in the miracle of revelation draw their scriptural support from John 13-17, a passage that is rich with language regarding the Holy Spirit.

These chapters describe the eve of Jesus' crucifixion, the last few hours of Jesus' life when He was alone with His twelve apostles. Several names of the people who were with Jesus are mentioned: Judas, Peter, John, Thomas, and Philip. All of these men were among Jesus' apostles. No one outside the apostles is mentioned from the time of the Last Supper in John 13 until Jesus' arrest in John 18.

Although the passage covers several chapters, it spans only a few hours. These were important hours for Jesus to speak with His apostles because they would be the last moments He could be alone with them before His death. Because He had to prepare them for His departure, He taught them several important truths about the Spirit on that evening. Was He speaking about only what the Spirit would do for the apostles, or do His teachings apply to all Christians today? What did Jesus really say about the Spirit?

After the Last Supper, when Jesus walked with His disciples toward the Mount of Olives where He would soon kneel in tearful prayer, Jesus comforted them, saying,

> Let not your hearts be troubled. Believe in God; believe also in me. In my Father's house are many rooms. If it were not so, would I have told you that I go to prepare a place for you? And if I go and prepare a place for you, I will come again and will take you to myself, that where I am you may be also. (John 14:1-3)

This passage may not mention the Spirit, but it does set the tone for the passages that follow. Jesus knew He was about to be killed and that the disciples would be alone without Him for the first time since they began following Him. He had just told them, "Yet a little while I am with you.... Where I am going you cannot come" (13:33). Peter asked, "Why can I not follow you now? I will lay down my life for you." Jesus replied, "Truly, truly I say to you, the cock will not crow till you have denied me three times" (13:37-38). Later Jesus will say, "...because I have said these things to you, sorrow has filled your heart" (16:6). You can see the continuity. These five chapters are a part of one long conversation on the Thursday night before Jesus was crucified. All that follows Jesus' encouragement at the beginning of John 14 is meant to comfort the disciples in the face of great sorrow and difficult trials.

The first reference to the Spirit comes in John 14:16-17:

> And I will ask the Father, and he will give you another Helper, to be with you forever, even the Spirit of truth, whom the world cannot receive, because it neither sees him nor knows him. You know him, for he dwells with you and will be in you.

The word "Helper" is translated from a word used only by John. In the Greek it is *parakletos*. It can also be translated "Comforter," "Advocate," or "Counselor." The word literally means "one who is called alongside." In 1 John 2:1 it obviously means "advocate." In Greek literature the word is used frequently to describe a legal advisor or helper or advocate in the courts. The point Jesus was making was that the apostles did not have to worry about Jesus' leaving them. He was sending Someone who would stand by them and help them.

This Helper was identified as the "Spirit of truth." The world cannot receive Him because it "neither sees him nor knows him," but the apostles were told that He would be "in" them.

Jesus developed the promise of the Spirit in verse 26: "But the Helper, the Holy Spirit, whom the Father will send in my name, he will teach you all things and bring to your remembrance all that I have said to you." As in verse 16, Jesus was again emphatic that the Father, not He, would send the Helper, but He would do it in Jesus' name.

The Spirit would help the apostles in two ways:

- "He will teach you all things." "All things" is not meant to encompass the full scope of human knowledge, but only those things related to the sphere of the apostles' work, those things related to "life and godliness" (2 Peter 1:3).
- "He will bring to your remembrance all that I have said to you." They would not need Bibles or notes or classes or even good memories. Something miraculous would occur in them to aid them in carrying out Jesus' mission after He was gone.

Jesus continued:

> Nevertheless, I tell you the truth: it is to your advantage that I go away, for if I do not go away, the Helper will not come to you. But if I go, I will send him to you. And when he comes, he will convict the world concerning sin and righteousness and judgment: concerning sin, because they do not believe in me; concerning righteousness, because I go to the Father, and you will see me no longer; concerning judgment, because the ruler of this world is judged. "I still have many things to say to you, but you cannot bear them now. When the Spirit of truth comes, he will guide you into all the truth, for he will not speak on his own authority, but whatever he hears he will speak, and he will declare to you the things that are to come. (John 16:7-13)

Jesus was encouraging them. It was to their "advantage" that He should leave so that the Helper could come (v. 7).

And when He came (upon the apostles), He would "convict" the world.

We use the word "convict" almost exclusively in the courts of law to refer to what happens when a jury finds someone guilty of a crime. In that situation, the laws of the land shine on the case to show a person's guilt. Here "convict" means to bring the light of truth to bear on what is wrong in the world, thus proving its guilt.

Jesus said the Spirit would convict the world regarding three things (vv. 8-11):

- "Sin." Jesus said the Spirit needed to convince the world of sin "because they do not believe in me."
- "Righteousness." He did not say "unrighteousness." The Helper's convictions are not negative. Jesus said the Spirit would teach the world righteousness "because I go to the Father." Jesus went to the Father by means of the cross. There is no righteousness without the cross!
- "Judgment." Jesus was not speaking of final judgment, but the judgment of "the ruler of this world," Satan. When Jesus "went away," the devil was judged and made powerless.

After speaking of the Spirit's work of conviction, there is a promise that sounds similar to what we read in John 14:26: "he will guide you into all the truth" (v. 13). Interestingly, this truth does not come by the Spirit's own authority, but "whatever he hears [from the Father] he will speak" (v. 13). This is very similar to what Jesus had earlier said of himself (14:10). Therefore, we should not make a distinction between the words of Jesus and the words of His disciples. They all come from the same source.

To Whom Was Jesus Speaking?
A number of learned Christian thinkers have applied these words to all believers. In 1938, N.B. Hardeman met a missionary Baptist named Ben Bogard for a public debate in Little Rock, Arkansas, covering the work of the Holy Spirit, the necessity of baptism, and other issues. One of the propositions defended by Bogard was, "The Scriptures teach that the sinner is so depraved that in his conviction and conversion the Holy Spirit exercises a power or influence, distinct from and in addition to the written word." One of the "Scriptures" he appealed to was John 13-17. At some point in the debate, Mr. Bogard said,

> Did you ever stop to think or to consider that Jesus said the Holy Spirit would come to take his place? Have you not read where Jesus said, "I will pray the Father, and he shall give you another Comforter, that he may abide with you forever?" (John 14:14-17) ...What I am affirming is that the Holy Spirit is personally present, is really present, in the conviction and conversion of the sinner as Jesus was present when he dealt with men and women while he was here in body, during his personal ministry.[1]

Bogard did not limit Jesus' words to the apostles. He believed all Christians should benefit from the Spirit's direct guidance.

One of the greatest apologists of our time is a man named William Lane Craig, author of a classic work on Apologetics entitled *Reasonable Faith*. He has debated the likes of Christopher Hitchens and Richard Dawkins. Sam Harris called him "the one Christian apologist who seems to have put the fear of God into all my fellow atheists." Craig's position on Apologetics is that arguments and evidence may be used to support the believer's faith, but the basis of faith is the "self-authenticating witness of God's Spirit who lives within him." After quoting John 14:26, Craig says,

> What John is talking about is the inner assurance the Holy Spirit gives of the basic truths of the Christian faith.... This assurance does not come from human arguments but directly from the Holy Spirit himself.[2]

Despite all the work Craig has done to show we can know God exists, even without using our Bibles, in the final analysis he does not believe a person can have faith unless God sends the Spirit to him just as He did to the apostles.

One of the bestselling Christian authors of our time is Francis Chan. He wrote a book called *Forgotten God* in which he urged readers to emphasize the Holy Spirit more in their lives. In the book he says, "...if you or I...had read only the Old and New Testaments, we would have significant expectations of the Holy Spirit in our lives." Then he goes to John 14, arguing that the Lord said "another Comforter" is coming and that He told His disciples it was to their "advantage" that He come. Then Chan says,

> If we read and believed these accounts, we would expect a great deal of the Holy Spirit. He would not be a mostly forgotten member of the Godhead whom we occasionally give a nod of recognition to.... We would expect our life with the Holy Spirit to look radically different from our old life without Him.[3]

Was Jesus speaking to all Christians? Remember the setting: Jesus was speaking with the twelve apostles alone after they had shared their last Passover feast together (cf. Matthew 26:20; Mark 14:17; Luke 22:14). These were the men whose feet were washed by Jesus. They were the ones who ate the Last Supper with Him. They were the ones among whom He first instituted the Lord's Supper.

If that isn't enough evidence to prove He was alone with the apostles, look carefully at some of the statements He made to those around Him:

- "Truly, truly, I say to you, whoever believes in me will also do the works that I do; and greater works than these will he do, because I am going to the Father" (John 14:12).
- "I have said all these things to you to keep you from falling away. They will put you out of the synagogues. Indeed, the hour is coming when whoever kills you will think he is offering service to God" (John 16:1-2).
- "A little while, and you will see me no longer; and again a little while, and you will see me" (John 16:16).
- "Behold, the hour is coming, indeed it has come, when you will be scattered, each to his own home, and will leave me alone. Yet I am not alone, for the Father is with me" (John 16:32).

Do these statements apply to all Christians today? If we can apply Jesus' promises regarding the Holy Spirit to the modern church, why not His prediction of "greater works" or His sad foreknowledge of being left alone?

There are other considerations that should lead us to believe that these statements about the Holy Spirit were not meant for us. For instance, why do those who claim to have this leading disagree on so many things? They disagree on the purpose of baptism, the mode of baptism, the role of women in worship, the organization of the church, and even the nature of God! How can one Spirit lead us in so many different directions?

In context, John 13-17 comprises Jesus' parting words to the apostles, not instructions to the 21st century church on the role of the Holy Spirit in the Christian's life.

Understandably, some will be uncomfortable with these conclusions. If Jesus was speaking only to the apostles, would we not also have to throw out passages like John 14:1-3 where Jesus reassures His disciples by promising them that He will go to prepare a place for them? While some of Jesus' promises apply to all Christians, others are meant for a select few. In the case of the Holy Spirit, the Bible plainly teaches that He works differently with us than He did in the early days. For example, Paul says, "As for prophecies, they will pass away; as for tongues, they will cease; as for [miraculous] knowledge, it will pass away" (1 Corinthians 13:8). God's gifts to the church today are "faith, hope, and love" (v. 13). Today the Spirit leads us, illuminates our hearts, and guides us, only He does this through the Word of God that He revealed to the inspired writers.

Jesus' promise of the Spirit was fulfilled in Acts 2. Before Jesus' ascension, He "ordered [the apostles] not to depart from Jerusalem, but to wait for the promise of the Father, which, he said, 'you heard from me, for John baptized with water, but you will be baptized with the Holy Spirit not many days from now" (Acts 1:4-5). Days later, they were baptized with the Spirit, just as Christ had said (Acts 2:1-4). From this point forward, the Spirit taught the apostles, brought everything to their remembrance, and guided them into all truth.

Some of the promises in John 13-17 have not been fulfilled, like the promise of many rooms in the Father's house. This was a broader promise including more people. The promises regarding the Spirit, however, have been fulfilled, leaving us with God's sufficient Word for a guide.

What About Us?
Just because Jesus was speaking directly to the apostles in John 13-17, that doesn't mean His words do not carry implications for us today. If Jesus had not gone away...

- The Father would not have sent the Spirit of truth, and if He had not done that...
- The apostles would not have been guided into all truth, and if they had not been guided into all truth...
- They would not have been able to preach the gospel and write it down in its present form in the New Testament, and if they had not done that...
- We would not know what Jesus did for us on the cross or how to receive God's grace so that we can be saved (cf. 2 Corinthians 6:1)!

All of that was done for us. Have you allowed the Spirit's help to benefit your soul?

NOTES

Chapter 1: The Focus of Faith
1. Leonore Shenazy, "Americans Long for a Chance to Rest, Replenish and Reboot," *Advertising Age* (November 12, 2008), 32.
2. Thom S. Ranier and Eric Geiger, *Simple Church* (B&H, 2006), 224.
3. Carl Spain, *The Letters of Paul to Timothy and Titus* (ACU Press, 1984), 28.
4. William D. Mounce, *Mounce's Expository Dictionary of Old & New Testament Words* (Zondervan, 2006), 439.
5. Paul Tillich, *Dynamics of Faith* (Harper & Row, 1957), 1.

Chapter 2: Faith without God
1. The KJV and others simply rendered the question: "Can faith save him?" In doing so, they fail to communicate the force of the adjective *tis*, which, along with the context, points to a distinct kind of faith, not faith in general.
2. John Calvin, *Institutes* (1.11).
3. Leo Tolstoy, *Anna Karenina* (The Bobbs-Merrill Co., Inc., 1901), 849.
4. Raymond Brown, *The Message of Hebrews* (InterVarsity Press, 1982), 13.
5. Quoted in Wayne Jackson, *The Bible and Science* (Courier Publications, 2000), 3.
6. Quoted in Wendell Berry, *Life Is a Miracle*, 16.
7. Berry, 19.
8. Quoted in Eric Metaxas, *Miracles* (Dutton, 2014), 25.

9. J.I. Packer, *Knowing God* (InterVarsity Press, 1973), 41.

Chapter 3: Faith without Knowledge
1. Quoted in David Lipe, "Faith and Knowledge," *Apologetics Press* (Apologetics Press, n.d.), 5.
2. Quoted in Kyle Butt, "Only True Christianity Is Defensible," *Apologetics Press*, www.apologeticspress.org/APContent.aspx?category=11&article=3585 (accessed September 10, 2015).
3. Ibid.
4. Quoted in Dick Sztanyo, *Graceful Reason* (Warren Christian Apologetics Center, 2012), 84-85.
5. Leo Tolstoy, *Anna Karenina* (The Bobbs-Merrill Co., Inc., 1901), 847.
6. C.S. Lewis, *Mere Christianity* (Macmillan, 1960), 31.
7. Thomas B. Warren and Antony G.N. Flew, *The Warren-Flew Debate on the Existence of God* (National Christian, 1977), 35-41.
8. Sztanyo, 81.

Chapter 4: Faith without Works
1. *Value Compact Edition, English Standard Version (ESV)* (Crossway, 2005), 899.
2. H.H. Price, "Belief 'In' and Belief 'That,'" *Religious Studies* (October, 1965), 5-27.
3. W.E. Vine, *Vine's Expository Dictionary of New Testament Words* (MacDonald Publishing Co., n.d.), 100.
4. Guy N. Woods, *The Epistle of James* (Gospel Advocate, 1964), 140.
5. Tom J. Nettles and Russell D. Moore, eds., *Why I Am a Baptist* (Broadman & Holman Publishers, 2001), 185.

6. Ibid., 158-9.
7. *Holy Bible*, Value Compact Edition, English Standard Version (Crossway, 2005), 899.

Chapter 5: The Reason for Miracles
1. R.C. Sproule, "Are Miracles for Today?" *Renewing Your Mind*, audio podcast.
2. William D. Mounce, *Mounce's Expository Dictionary of Old & New Testament Words* (Zondervan, 2006), 452.
3. C.S. Lewis, "Miracles," *The Grand Miracle and Other Selected Essays on Theology and Ethics from* God in the Dock (ed. Walter Hooper; Ballantine Books, 1970), 4-5.
4. Richard C. Trench, *Notes on the Miracles of Our Lord* (Fleming H. Revell Co., 1953), 290.
5. Lewis, 5.
6. Horatio Gates Spafford, "It Is Well with My Soul," *Songs of Faith and Praise* (Howard Publishing Co., 1994), 490.
7. For another passage where Paul discusses the end of the miraculous age, see Ephesians 4:11-16. Paul argues that God gave some miracle-working leaders, such as apostles and prophets, to the church "until we all attain to the unity of the faith and of the knowledge of the Son of God." Here, "the faith" is used in the sense of the Word of God (cf. Jude 3). Miracles of revelation were given to the church until the time when the Word was "united," or brought together. That being done, miracles would no longer be needed.

Chapter 6: A Believer's Unbelief
1. Robert E. Egner and Lester E. Denonn, ed., "Why I Am Not a Christian," *The Basic Writings of Bertrand Russell* (Simon & Schuster, 1961), 593.
2. Timothy Keller, *King's Cross* (Dutton, 2011), 120.
3. John Franklin Carter, quoted in David Roper, *Life of Christ, 1* (Resource Publications, 2003), 557.
4. Quoted in Roper, 552.
5. J.W. McGarvey, *Matthew and Mark* (Gospel Light Publishing Co., 1875), 818.
6. Herbert Lockyer, *All the Miracles of the Bible* (Zondervan, 1961), 216.
7. McGarvey, 153.
8. Richard C. Trench, *Notes on the Miracles of the Bible* (Fleming H. Revell Co.1953), 403.

Chapter 7: Long Distance Healing
1. John R. Wreford, "When My Love to Christ Grows Weak," *Songs of Faith and Praise* (Howard Publishing Co., 1994), 350.
2. R.C. Trench, *Notes on the Miracles of Our Lord* (Fleming H. Revell Co., 1953), 132.
3. J.W. McGarvey and Philip Y. Pendleton, *The Fourfold Gospel* (Standard Publishing, n.d.), 158.
4. Ibid., 157.

Chapter 8: Walking Trees
1. Henry E. Turlington, *Mark* (The Broadman Bible Commentary, vol. 8; Broadman Press, 1969), 333.
2. James A. Brooks, *Mark* (The American Commentary; Broadman Press, 1991), 132.
3. R.C.H. Lenski, *The Interpretation of St. Mark's Gospel*, (The Wartburg Press, 1946), 329.

4. Pliny the Elder, *The Natural History* (28:7).
5. Ronald L. Eisenberg, "8 Popular Jewish Superstitions," *My Jewish Learning*, www.myjewishlearning.com/article/popular-superstitions/ (accessed January 18, 2018).
6. Lenski, 330.
7. Richard C. Trench, *Notes on the Miracles of the Bible* (Fleming H. Revell Co.1953), 391.

Chapter 9: The Man Who Had Died

1. R.C.H. Lenski, *The Interpretation of St. John's Gospel* (Hendrickson Publishers, 2001), 798.
2. Raymond E. Brown, *The Gospel According to John I-XII*, (The Anchor Bible; Doubleday, 1966), 433.
3. A.T. Robertson, *Robertson's Word Pictures of the New Testament*, www.biblestudytools.com/commentaries/robertsons-word-pictures/john/john-11-33.html (accessed March 2, 2018).
4. Walter Bauer, F.W. Danker, William F. Arndt, and F. Wilbur Gingrich, *A Greek-English Lexicon of the New Testament and Other Early Christian Literature* (2nd ed.; U Chicago P, 1979), 254.
5. Lenski, 807-8.
6. Randy Alcorn, *Heaven* (Tyndale, 2004), 281.

Chapter 10: The Inspiration of the Bible

1. C.S. Lewis, Mere Christianity (McMillan Publishing Co., 1943), 56.
2. Norman L. Geisler and William E. Nix, *General Introduction to the Bible*, 39.
3. Lee Strobel, *The Case for Faith* (Zondervan, 2000), 129.

Chapter 11: How to Study the Bible

1. John Maxwell, *Today Matters* (Warner Faith, 2004), 67.
2. Jeff Fearnside, "Digging In: Wendell Berry On Small Farms, Local Wisdom, And The Folly Of Greed," *The Sun* (July 2008), www.thesunmagazine.org/issues/391/digging-in (accessed March 2, 2018).
3. Albert Mohler, "The Scandal of Biblical Illiteracy: It's Our Problem," *Albert Mohler* (January 20, 2016), https://albertmohler.com/2016/01/20/the-scandal-of-biblical-illiteracy-its-our-problem-4/ (accessed March 2, 2018).
4. Ed Stetzer, "The Epidemic of Bible Illiteracy in Our Churches," *Christianity Today* (July 6, 2015), www.christianitytoday.com/edstetzer/2015/july/epidemic-of-bible-illiteracy-in-our-churches.html (accessed March 2, 2018).
5. John Piper, *Think* (Crossway, 2010), 41.
6. Timothy Keller, *Prayer* (Dutton 2014), 50.
7. Ibid., 90.
8. A great resource for translations and word studies is www.blueletterbible.com. Also, check out www.apologeticspress.org for articles on Apologetics.
9. Harrell Davidson, *Over the Vast Horizon: Authorized Biography of Guy N. Woods* (Obion, 2003), p. 171.

Chapter 12: Obedience through Suffering

1. See the appendix for a detailed discussion of the Spirit's work in revealing God's will.
2. Marvin W. Meyer, *Who Do People Say I Am?* (Eerdmans, 1983), 69.

3. Isaac Watts, "When I Survey the Wondrous Cross," *Songs of Faith and Praise* (Howard Publishing Co., 1994), 315.
4. *Archaeological Study Bible* (Zondervan, 2005), 1612.
5. John R.W. Stott, *The Cross of Christ* (Inter-Varsity Press, 1986), 73.
6. *Ibid.*
7. *Ibid.*
8. *Ibid.*
9. Joseph C. Clements, "Medical Aspects of the Crucifixion of Jesus Christ," *When I Survey the Wondrous Cross* (Faulkner University, 1992), 107.
10. Raymond Brown, *The Message of Hebrews: Christ above All* (Inter-Varsity, 1982), 99.
11. Stott, 76.
12. "The State of the Church 2016," *Barna*, www.barna.com/research/state-church-2016/ (accessed March 12, 2018).
13. Greg Ogden, *Transforming Discipleship* (Inter-Varsity Press, 2003), 46-7.
14. Brown, 101.
15. Jeffrey C. Johnson, "The Vale of Soul Making," *The Paris Review* (July 25, 2014), www.theparisreview.org/blog/2014/07/25/the-vale-of-soul-making/ (accessed April 2, 2015).

Chapter 13: Planting Faith

1. George Barna and David Kinnaman, *Churchless* (Tyndale, 2014), Loc 2055.
2. Ibid., Loc 467.
3. Ibid., Loc 2079.
4. Ibid., Loc 2344.
5. Ibid., Loc 2354.

Appendix: The Holy Spirit
1. Ben M. Bogard, First Affirmative Speech, "The Work of the Holy Spirit," *Hardeman-Bogard Debate* (Gospel Advocate, 1938), 9.
2. Quoted in Dick Sztanyo, *Graceful Reason* (Warren Christian Apologetics Center, 2012), 295.
3. Francis Chan and Danae Yankoski, *Forgotten God* (David Cook, 2009), 29-30.

also available through
Riddle Creek Publishing

To the Overcomers by Andy Kizer
Make Your Stand by Drew Kizer
Wisdom's Call by Drew Kizer
Be Wise God's Way by Adam Faughn
The Cast of the Cross by Drew Kizer
From Slaves to Conquerors by Barton Kizer
Marriage and the Christian Home by Dr. Ted Burleson
Who Knew? Records of Divine Providence by Andy Kizer
From Conquerors to Kings by Drew Kizer
The Fifteen Periods of Bible History by Andy Kizer
Christian Hope by Drew Kizer
Dangerous Playground by Drew Kizer

Riddle Creek Pocket Guides

Five Class Sessions Each Guide

"Psalms and the Issues"
"Instructions for Successful Living"
"Families with a Focus"

Useful tools for camp counselors, youth ministers, retreat leaders, and Bible class teachers.

Made in the USA
Coppell, TX
18 March 2020